J. M. (John Moore) Capes

The Mosaic-worker's daughter

Vol. I

J. M. (John Moore) Capes

The Mosaic-worker's daughter
Vol. I

ISBN/EAN: 9783337040857

Printed in Europe, USA, Canada, Australia, Japan

Cover: Foto ©ninafisch / pixelio.de

More available books at **www.hansebooks.com**

THE MOSAIC-WORKER'S DAUGHTER.

A NOVEL.

BY

J. M. CAPES.

IN THREE VOLUMES.
VOL. I.

LONDON:
RICHARD BENTLEY, NEW BURLINGTON STREET.
1868.

[*All rights reserved.*]

CONTENTS OF VOL. I.

CHAPTER	PAGE
I. HELEN; MARGARET; FRANCESCA	1
II. THE BALL AT THE FRENCH EMBASSY	24
III. ESCAPED	50
IV. MORNING VISITORS	68
V. D'URBINO IN HIS STUDIO	89
VI. THE GATHERING IN THE COLISEUM	107
VII. THE ARRIVAL AND ITS RESULTS	123
VIII. ARRESTED	143
IX. WITHIN AND WITHOUT THE POLICE COURT	168
X. MR. EVELYN'S ACCOUNT OF HIMSELF	193
XI. DONATO	209
XII. FATHER AND DAUGHTER	226
XIII. THE MARCHESE MAKES ENQUIRIES	247
XIV. LONELINESS	269

THE MOSAIC-WORKER'S DAUGHTER.

CHAPTER I.

HELEN; MARGARET; FRANCESCA.

"Only three weeks yet in Rome, and two invitations to balls already!"

"Yes!" said Helen Sandford, to her friend and cousin Margaret Osborne; "everybody says that we are to have a gayer season than ever, this winter."

"But as to these Roman balls themselves," asked Margaret, "I cannot understand what sort of affairs they can possibly be."

"Why so?" asked her cousin.

"Surely I have heard both you and my

aunt say again and again that the Roman girls are hardly ever allowed to dance, or even to appear at any large assemblies, until they are actually married."

"So much the worse for the Roman girls, and for both Roman and English gentlemen," replied Helen. "But at the same time, so much the better for us English girls. You have not an idea what a sensation you yourself will produce next week, when you come floating into a crowd of young dukes and princes, with your bright locks and the roses and lilies of your cheeks. Do you know that the young Romans are wild about complexions like yours? As for me, with my dark face and dark eyes and dark hair, they think me no better than one of their own inane and ignorant sisters."

"Really?" asked her cousin. "If this is not one of your favourite exaggerations, Helen, it only proves the stupidity of your friends the dukes and the princes."

"The proof is before you, my dear," replied

Helen. "This is my third Roman winter, and I am still Helen Sandford, and for all that has yet taken place, likely so still to remain."

"But I thought that these youthful nobles were all anxious to marry English girls."

"Not all of them, by any means, nor half of them, unless these same English girls have pretty fortunes as well as pretty eyes."

"Yet you have both of these charms, Helen."

"True enough," she said; "but nevertheless I am Helen Sandford still. And I am told, moreover, that I frightened the butterflies away, by exposing their ignorance in all sorts of subjects that are perfectly well understood by young Englishmen of the same station."

"And do you admit this explanation of their insensibility?" asked Margaret.

"It is not only the opinion of my mother herself," said Helen. "It is the opinion of my old playfellow Henry Noel as well."

"Do you mean to say that my aunt discusses such delicate subjects as your marriage prospects with Mr. Noel, or with any other person whatsoever?"

"Why not?" asked Helen. "Mr. Noel is no longer young; and besides, being in orders, he is a perfectly unbiased adviser; and is, I am convinced, most anxious for my happiness."

"Well!" rejoined Margaret; "It seems rather an odd sort of proceeding, to my English notions of propriety!"

"When you have lived abroad as much as I have, Margaret," said Helen, "you will have given up this and a good many other insular prejudices into the bargain."

"You think so?" asked Margaret.

"I am sure of it," rejoined Helen.

"Possibly!" said Margaret, with something very much like a sigh; "but the prospect is scarcely a pleasant one."

And she walked to the window, and looked out upon the scene below, wondering whether the new life on which she was now entering would prove as bright and happy as she had been expecting it to be. The house whence she now watched a sight strangely novel to her, was situated in one of those streets near the Piazza di Spagna, where wealthy British parents love to settle themselves for the Roman winter, and thence, as a base of operations, pursue the campaign of mingled pleasure and piety on which they have set their eager hearts.

What are the relative proportions of the motives which tempt them to the Eternal City it is not easy to decide. With Protestant travellers, except those of the extreme high-church school, pleasure alone is the avowed object of the visit, their pious aspirations being abundantly satisfied by a full-dress attendance on Sundays at the thoroughly non-ritual service which Roman jealousy allows to be performed without the walls, and without the walls alone. Catholics, on the other hand, persuade themselves that it is piety, far more than pleasure-seeking, which prompts them to come on a sort of pilgrimage to the feet of the Holy Father; an agreeable illusion which Roman ecclesiastics are careful to foster, and which thus furnishes one practical matter in which the Roman shopkeepers are of the same mind as their spiritual masters.

Mrs. Sandford and her daughters being now entering upon their third season, were thoroughly disillusionised as to the nature of their motives.

They had returned to their old quarters with precisely the same views that bring the crowds of the rich and fashionable to London every spring.

With Margaret the case was different. The long-continued illnesses of her father and mother, followed by their deaths, had grafted an almost premature gravity on a character naturally buoyant; and she had come to Italy under the shelter of her aunt's protection, prepared to find herself in harmony with the grandeurs of the Rome of the past, and the splendours of the Rome of the present, rather than with the brilliant gaieties which she saw were already beginning to pall upon her cousin's energetic and thoroughly honest mind.

For some minutes she sat and watched the stream of people below, noting once more how unlike it all seemed to the stream that flowed up and down the streets of London. To her unaccustomed eye the novelty of Roman life had not yet worn off, and though at their hours of greatest bustle, the streets and squares were never thronged with eager, grave and busy-looking crowds, like those with which the Londoner is familiar from his earliest years, yet the vivacity of the Italian voices, and the gesticulations with which all Italians accompany their ordinary talk, gave a life to the common aspect of every day affairs which would be sought in vain in the damp atmosphere and under the gloomy skies of the north.

Presently her attention was fixed upon a sight altogether new and strange. Two figures advanced slowly up the street, clad from head to foot in white cloaks, with their faces completely hidden by white masks, pierced with two holes to allow them to see where they were going. Anything so grotesque and ghastly-looking Margaret had never beheld, except upon the stage in a Christmas pantomime. That they were some sort of beggars was soon evident. Before the door of every house they paused and silently held out the bags they carried, one taking the houses on the right side of the street, the other those on the left. At almost every house something that seemed a coin was dropped into the bags by one of the inmates, in return for which the recipient made a profound bow, but said nothing, and walked on.

"Helen! Helen!" cried Margaret, as the

strange pair came nearer, " here are the most wonderful looking beggars you can conceive of. They will be stopping here in a moment. What are we to say to them?"

"Nothing at all. Rome swarms with beggars of all sort," replied Helen, her curiosity quite unpiqued.

"But these are not common beggars surely," rejoined Margaret, "common beggars do not go about in white cloaks and masks, unless they want to frighten people into parting with their money."

"It's only the *Sacconi*," replied Helen, totally unimpressed by her cousin's surprise.

"And who are the *Sacconi*, then?" asked Margaret.

"Oh! I forgot it was your first winter here," said Helen. "The *Sacconi* are a society of lay and clerical swells who disguise themselves, and go about collecting alms for poor debtors. I daresay these two men that you see coming are Princes or Cardinals. It won't do to give them nothing; but a few *bajocchi* will be quite enough. Just call Fernando, as you seem to be doing nothing, and tell him to be ready at the door with the money."

"Does Aunt Sandford really like this sort of thing, Helen?" asked Margaret, slightly bewildered at the notion of cardinals and nobles masquerading in the cause of charity.

"I don't know whether she likes it or not; but she would not like to be singular, you know, in anything," rejoined Helen.

Margaret said no more, but found herself already imitating the characteristic Roman shrug of the shoulders, and straightway left the room in search of Fernando, the *ci-devant* courier, and now the butler and general factotum of the Sandford party.

Fernando, however, was not immediately forthcoming; so Margaret ran down stairs herself, anxious to catch a near sight of the mysterious pair of pious maskers. As she reached the door, one of the cloaked figures was holding out his bag to the owner of the adjoining house, a worker in mosaic, who supplied some of the chief dealers in that pretty Roman manufacture, and also sold what he could on his own account at home. She had already made the acquaintance of this man, Filippo Giorgione by name, partly through her admiration of his ingenuity as an artist-mechanic, and partly through a fancy she had taken for his handsome daughter Francesca.

Neither the masked figure nor Giorgione caught sight of her for a few moments, and she had time to see that what the mosaic-worker dropped into the bag of the *Sacconi* was certainly a small piece of paper, whether containing money or not she of course could not tell. She was confident, moreover, that the look of the brilliant eyes that shot through the holes in the mask meant something more than the mere routine gratitude for a trifling gift; and that the usual solemn reverence with which the gift was acknowledged was responded to by a scarcely perceptible curl of the lips of the donor.

It was all over in some twenty or thirty seconds, but the conviction which flashed upon Margaret's mind was immediately strengthened by the change of manner in the two men, when they caught sight of her, and the bag was duly presented for her expected gift. The change was barely perceptible, but she was so convinced that it was real, that after bestowing the prescribed number of bajocchi, and receiving the appropriate reverence in return, she determined to stay and gossip for a few minutes with her friend the mosaic-worker. She was already well aware that being an English girl she could do such a thing with impunity, and with no damage to her reputation, though to a Roman girl of her social position such independence in action is still rigorously forbidden.

"How is Francesca this morning?" she asked of the father, after acknowledging his salutation, given with all that pleasant cordiality and polished manner, in which we

English people of almost every class have yet so much to learn from the Italians.

"The signora is most kind and considerate," said Giorgione. "Francesca is here to answer for herself, though she keeps within doors, as the day is still rather chilly for one who is not yet quite recovered from illness."

"Chilly!" echoed Margaret, as she preceded Giorgione into his working room. "I find it quite delightful in comparison with our English Decembers."

"Ah, well!" said Giorgione, "it is happy for us Romans that all the good things should not be monopolised by the signora's excellent fellow-countrymen. We have the sun, which is the light of the body. But the English have liberty, which is the light of the soul. It would be terrible if we had neither the one nor the other."

"But what a wonderful place this Rome of yours really is," returned Margaret. "Every day I come upon some fresh thing that astonishes me. Just now I am bewildered by the apparition of these mysterious gentlemen in the masks and cloaks. Is it really true that they are nobles, and bishops, and cardinals? I noticed, too, that they are walking about with bare feet. Such a thing would be stopped in London by the police for good and all."

"Who knows?" replied the mosaic-worker, with a shrug and a grimace, that left Margaret more puzzled than ever. "But here is Francesca," he continued, "waiting to give an account of herself. The signora will pardon me if I return to my work."

And with a low bow, he took his departure, while Francesca came forward to greet her visitor.

She was one of those girls often seen in many parts of Italy, but rarely on the northern side of the Alps.

Few things, it is true, are more striking from the Alps to Sicily, than the variations in the looks of the women. Taken as a whole, and including the people of the Abruzzi, and other similar districts famed for female ugliness, the average beauty of Italian girls is perhaps not higher than the average of English women. But as it is not uncommon to see Italian girls of an unquestionable degree of plainness, which is comparatively rare in England, developing itself into a positive hideousness as they grow old, especially among the poor, so, by way of compensation, it is not unusual to meet with Italian girls—not only among the nobles and the more cultivated classes, but among the peasantry themselves—possessed of beauty of feature of the highest order, and recalling the perfections of form which we recognise in the finest works of Greek and Roman sculpture.

Francesca Giorgione was one of these superb examples of the living ideal. Her father, who was a connoisseur in pictures as well as a kind of artist himself, would now and then protest that she must inherit the blood as well as the name of the famous Giorgione, so thoroughly was she a representative of the gorgeous style of beauty most loved by the great Venetian.

It was only a fancy of his own, it is true, but he talked so often about the pleasant fiction, that he was sometimes rallied on having come almost to believe in it as a fact; at any rate, it might be a fact, he was wont to assert, for as he knew nothing of his own ancestors beyond his great-grandfather, nobody could deny the possibility of the descent, in the absence of all proof against it.

To those who are familiar with the grand and statuesque type of countenance of the true Italian kind, there would be nothing strange in Francesca's face and its expression. To the English, French, or German critic, who has neither crossed the Alps nor made himself familiar with the pictures of Giorgione, and the other masters of the superb Venetian school, it is difficult to describe such a countenance, and the lights that beam from it.

At once grand and statuesque, it is at the same time perfectly feminine and mobile. The fulness of the lips is rich and sensuous, but by no means necessarily voluptuous. The nose and the chin are boldly cut and solid, when compared with the profile of English women of undoubted beauty, but the tenderness of the eyes, and the rapid movements of the mouth neutralise all suggestions of heaviness and masculine hardness. Except in rare cases, impulse speaks in every movement of the lips, and every glance of the large full eyes; and even when the clear, brown complexion has no tint of carmine when in a condition of repose, the flush that accompanies every excitement adds all that charm of colour, without which we English people are apt to think the noblest face deficient in life and loveliness.

Upon Margaret herself, Francesca's face

was beginning to exercise quite a strange fascination. The more she talked to her—and scarcely a day passed without her coming in for a half-hour's gossip—the more deeply she felt interested in her history, and the more she wondered as to the destiny which might be in store for a girl, in whom the capacity for loving was plainly accompanied with an equal capacity for suffering. What latent depths of passionate emotions lay hidden within her heart, Margaret of course could only surmise; but that she was a person of no common-place character was perfectly clear.

Like most Italians, she was more at her ease with persons whom she recognised as her social superiors than is the case with English girls of the same class. Nevertheless, Margaret had a suspicion that she secretly fretted against the barriers set up by rank and wealth to keep back the plebeian and the poor from any real equality with those more fortunate than themselves, to a degree that seemed out of harmony with the manifest strength of her general mind and character.

This morning she seemed more than ordinarily grave and absent, and to find no enjoyment in correcting the small errors in her visitor's pronunciation of Italian, which, by Margaret's own desire, she was in the habit of noting. Like the Romans of almost every rank, Francesca spoke with the pure flowing *bocca Romana*, though grammatically her Italian had less of the real *lingua Toscana* than the accurate phrases of the well-taught Margaret.

"Do you never do anything in the mosaic way yourself, Francesca?" asked Margaret, after inquiring into the convalescent's health. "It seems just the sort of work for a woman's hands. I must have some lessons from your father myself, I think."

"Sometimes," replied Francesca; "but it's not an occupation I care about."

"Why so? It must be pleasanter than

the mere using the fingers in common needlework."

"That is just why it does not suit me at all. It neither leaves me quite free to think, nor gives me quite enough to think about."

"But surely," asked Margaret, surprised at the habit of self-analysis which the girl's answer implied, "surely your thoughts are not always so eager or so far away, that they cannot fix themselves on the arranging of these pretty little strips and threads of glass? It is glass; is it not?"

"Yes; so they call it, and so I suppose it is. But it is a fidgetting work, nevertheless. I can understand painting a picture, but this is neither a mere labour nor an absorbing pleasure. Is it a favourite with young ladies in England, signorina?"

"I am afraid that our fashionable English amusements are far more worthless," replied Margaret.

"I don't understand England," observed

the girl; "I wish I did. Is it true that all people are equal in England, and that the nobles can marry the girls of the *mezzo ceto*, or even the peasant girls, if they choose?"

"If they choose, they certainly can," rejoined Margaret, "but the feeling of the country is so much against it, that it rarely happens; and when it does, it usually turns out ill."

"If we had liberty here, do you think rich people would marry the poor?" asked Francesca, speaking in a dreamy, half-absent manner, as if anxious to make her question seem a mere piece of trivial inquisitiveness.

"No, never!" rejoined Margaret. "Nowhere in the world is equality practised to such an extent as that."

"But they tell us that in England everybody can read and write; and so all people are quite equal."

"Oh! Francesca!" cried Margaret, "who has been deluding you with such wonderful stories? Besides, as to reading, you read a good deal yourself, do you not?"

"Just my prayer book, but not very much more," said Francesca; "and there's not much in that, is there, signorina?" she added, producing a well-thumbed little volume, and putting it into Margaret's hand. Like the rest of her class, Francesca found her devotional feelings stimulated more by pictures than by printed prose, and accordingly the book was crowded with the little pious engravings of saints and angels, which the fastidious critic finds so ludicrously ugly, but in which the zealous Catholic finds so much edification. As Margaret turned the leaves over carelessly, her attention was caught by the photograph of a head, presenting a surprising contrast to its companion prints.

"Who is this?" she asked. "There is no name to it, but I should hardly fancy it is the face of a saint at all. If it is, I never saw sanctity look so uncommonly stern in my life before. But the features themselves are wonderfully fine," she continued, studying them carefully.

"I have seen the same features looking full of love and sweetness," rejoined Francesca, gazing fixedly before her, as if in a half-dream. Nothing more, however, could Margaret extract from her, without a closeness of questioning from which she shrank, as an impertinence; and after a few feeble attempts at conversation on other matters, she left the mosaic-worker's daughter to her solitary thoughts.

CHAPTER II.

THE BALL AT THE FRENCH EMBASSY.

The night of the ball soon arrived, when Margaret was to learn for the first time how like, and yet in some respects how unlike, is a Roman to a London ball. It was not, indeed, a genuine Roman ball, being given by the French ambassador's wife, and it was somewhat less exclusive than the gatherings at the palaces of the oldest Roman nobles, and still less exclusive than the balls given by those more modern dukes and princes, who are stigmatised by the older patrician houses as the *nobiltá del Papa.*

And curious and significant it is to trace the excessive slowness with which the ideas of modern life permeate a social system, like that of Rome, founded upon ideas now dying out all over the world. Intensely democratic as is the influence of the Papacy, so far as it allows the tiara to be worn by men who have sprung from the humblest ranks of the people; nevertheless its tendency to ally itself with kings and nobles, and to force its adherents into its ranks, entirely neutralises all its popular elements. Accordingly, scarcely in Spain, or in the more oligarchical districts of Germany, is the contempt of the old nobility for the new creations more distinctly understood, or more openly avowed, than it is in Rome. The Popes, say the haughty inheritors of ancient names, can make their nephews and their bankers into dukes and princes; but can they confer a lineage running up to the old Roman patricians, or even to the turbulent middle ages, when the Italian nobles were the only living powers in the land?

Nevertheless, if the ball at the French

embassy betrayed the incursion of social ideas from which oligarchical mediævalism would have recoiled, it exhibited the solid advantages of the new system so pleasantly, that the very bluest of blood must have blushed into crimson warmth at the contrast with its own shortcomings. Already Margaret had made acquaintance with the interior of one or two splendid-looking palaces, and had learnt to anticipate a scene in which the guests might be very well-bred, while the rooms were very miserable, and the eating and drinking reduced to a minimum. Here, however, in place of a dingy, ill-kept and even dirty staircase, whose breadth of size and marble construction suggested only the ambition of its builder and the poverty of his successors, Mrs. Sandford, with her daughter and her niece, found themselves in the midst of a scene which made them fancy themselves back again in Paris. Lights, flowers, carpetings, attendants, music, and abundance of all such dainties for the soothing of the palate as Rome could supply or France could export, assured them that if the ancestry of the hosts dated only from the Napoleonic era, their purse and their tastes were of even a more modern creation.

Hosts of salutations, all tolerably cordial, greeted Mrs. Sandford and Helen, while Helen herself, half-pleased and half-envious, witnessed the instantaneous fulfilment of her prophecies as to the effect of her cousin's appearance upon a susceptible race, like the young men of "birth and fashion" in modern Rome. Both girls were speedily provided with partners, not only pleasant men to talk with, but one of them eminently "eligible" in the eyes of an experienced matron like Mrs. Sandford. "Be cautious! my dear," she whispered in her daughter's ear, as Helen moved from her side; while Margaret, who overheard the advice, well knew what it meant, and wondered how far it would be obeyed. When the dance was over, the cousins and their partners formed a little group around Mrs. Sandford, and began to talk.

"Ah! Marchese!" said Helen, offering her hand, with true English freedom, to Margaret's late partner; "I am delighted to see you already cultivating my cousin's acquaintance. I trust you have pardoned my *brusqueries* of last winter."

"That which would be *brusquerie* in one of our Romans," replied the Marchese Della Porta, "is but pleasant vivacity in the fair daughters of England."

"Then you have forgiven my laughing at your Roman notions of sport, I hope," said Helen. "Do you know what is here called sport, Margaret?" she added, turning to her cousin.

"Pardon me, Miss Osborne," interrupted the gentleman, "if I venture to contradict, or rather to modify or explain the censure implied in Miss Sandford's question. We are now giving up the old fashions, and borrowing your English ways."

"Yes! Marchese!" broke in Helen's late partner; adding, in a low voice, "in sport at least it is permitted to us to become men."

"Perhaps, as the old fashion is going out, you will tell me what it was that my cousin used to laugh at," interposed Margaret.

"Only this?" exclaimed Helen, before either Della Porta, or his acquaintance, could reply. "Only this, that a wretched owl used to be tied to a stake in the daylight; and as he fluttered about in his misery, a host of small birds came down and pecked at their helpless enemy, while the gentlemen sportsmen stood by, and shot the unlucky birds; thus combining manly sport with forethought for the next day's dinner."

A barely perceptible frown and gleam from the eyes betrayed the irritation that the sarcastic speech awoke in the Marchese's acquaintance, who was now formally introduced to Margaret, as the Cavaliere d'Urbino, and who at once secured her hand for the waltz that was about to begin.

"Your cousin is a little hard upon us," said he, as they began to move in a slow, measured, circling sweep, suggested by the singularly floating and almost complaining melody which the musicians struck up, and which passed muster as a waltz.

"You must pardon her, Cavaliere," replied Margaret. "You must put it down to our uncouth insular ways, and not to any want of real heart and feeling."

He said nothing for a minute or so; then in quite another tone, he asked her what she thought of the melody to which they were dancing.

"As a melody, it is lovely," she answered, "but as a dance is it not rather strange?"

"Look to the other end of the room," replied D'Urbino, almost in a whisper; "but let no one see you are looking. Do you notice that tall, handsome man, in a rather remarkable dress, or rather uniform? Give a glance at his face, as we pass near him, but for Heaven's sake without seeming to notice him, and then I will explain all about the music."

A few more turns in the dance brought them near the person thus pointed out, and as they passed him Margaret took in his whole figure at a glance. Whether he was a soldier or not, she could not decide from his dress, and he had scarcely enough of that military air and *abandon* which is either natural or assumed in the officers of European armies in general. His countenance was perfectly impassive, as he stood listening to the gossip of two or three acquaintances. He appeared not even to notice Margaret and her partner, as they floated past him; but with all their unmoved calm, the repose of his features seemed to her to be the result of habitual effort rather than of the quietness of the mind within him.

"You noticed him?" inquired Margaret's companion, as soon as they were well out of earshot.

"I should have noticed him, whether you had given the hint or not," she replied. "But what has he to do with the music?"

"This waltz, or whatever they call it, is a forbidden thing in Rome, being really a patriotic song, which our paternal masters have decided to be unfit for the lips of their affectionate children. We hear it to-night, because as you know, a foreign embassy is a privileged spot; and there are more than two of the musicians who would chant it up and down the Corso, if they dared."

"But what has your handsome friend to do with it?" she asked.

"My friend, indeed!" he echoed. "Ah! if you knew all. But you are only jesting, I know. If you go out much this season, you will soon learn that it is possible for a man to have innumerable acquaintances, but no friends."

"Do you speak of yourself?" feeling as if she was getting unpleasantly involved in the confidences of a perfect stranger, but led on by an irresistible mixture of curiosity and fascination.

"Myself? No, indeed," he rejoined. "It is Rinaldo who has no friends, but acquaintances everywhere. But I forgot. I had not told you his name. Signor Giovanni Rinaldo holds one of those posts about the Court which some of our nobles, and many others, are not ashamed to hold, and even to seek for. He is one of the *cameriere di spada*, who think it an honour to swell the train of the Holy Father, as it is still the fashion to call him."

"Is that all?" asked Margaret.

His reply was at first only a shrug, accompanied with that expressive look, partly cynical, partly acquiescent, which is in such favour with not a few men of all classes all over Italy, and, more than anywhere else, in Rome itself. Then the dance came to an end, and Margaret sat down a little apart from the crowd, while D'Urbino, apologising gracefully for the liberty, seated himself sufficiently near her to keep up the conversation in a somewhat subdued tone.

"But why," continued he, "should I make a mystery of what you will be sure to hear whispered over and over again, and perhaps before this very evening is over? Rinaldo has the reputation of being a spy, acting in the interests of our clerical and despotic Government; and what that means you can readily guess!"

"A spy," she echoed, with undisguised astonishment. "But is he a gentleman? and how comes he here if this is the story told of him?"

"The innocent, Miss Osborne," rejoined D'Urbino, speaking, to her surprise, in very tolerable English, "never suspect vice and crime, unless forced upon their notice, and to an Englishwoman it seems incredible that one who is a gentleman should play the traitor, and yet mix freely in the society of honourable men and women."

"But is it certain that the charge is true?" she asked.

"It is impossible to prove anything at all in Rome," he replied. "No! there is no actual proof of it; but the suspicion is universal among us Liberals, and even the most honest of the Papalini themselves distrust him."

"And he is asked everywhere in society?" asked Margaret.

"Of course; why not? If nobody was visited by anybody about whom there is some suspicion, society would come to an end, and be simply annihilated."

"A most miserable state of things, indeed!" exclaimed Margaret. "And as you must have noticed in England, such a condition of society would be to us utterly intolerable."

"I have never been in England," observed D'Urbino, surprised.

"Never?" asked Margaret. "You speak English remarkably well, then; and I cannot persuade myself that I have never met you before."

"Impossible," he answered. "I have never been in England, and we cannot have met in Rome, for I only came back this afternoon, and I have been, for the last month, in Venice."

Then rising from his seat, he continued in Italian, and in a voice no longer suppressed, "Then I shall have the pleasure of bringing you the photographs of San Marco and the Bridge of Sighs in the course of to-morrow morning, if Mrs. Sandford will permit me."

Utterly bewildered at his change of voice and manner, and at the mention of the photographs, of which not a word had hitherto been said, Margaret was unable to reply; when turning her head slightly round, the approaching figure of Rinaldo furnished a key to the puzzle; and she listened with apparent composure and interest to D'Urbino, as he proceeded to dilate on the beauties of photographs taken under the Italian sunlight. As he still spoke, Rinaldo was at his side, and the two men saluted one another with cold but not ungraceful courtesy.

"I have the permission of Mrs. Sandford," Rinaldo began, "to beg Signor D'Urbino to introduce me to Miss Osborne, who, if I mistake not, is one of our newest visitors."

Showing no signs of surprise, D'Urbino at once accomplished the introduction, and Rinaldo continued:—

"I can assure Miss Osborne that the Cavaliere D'Urbino is no mean judge in all matters of art. I think I heard Venetian photographs mentioned as I came up just now."

"Signor D'Urbino was pointing out the influence of the brilliant Italian sun in giving them a sharpness and delicacy impossible in our colder latitudes," rejoined Margaret.

"And there is no place in the world like Venice, for supplying subjects for the sun to make his pictures," remarked Rinaldo.

"I hope some day to see Venice under the sun itself;" said Margaret.

"It looks better in the photograph than in the reality," observed D'Urbino.

"How so?" asked Margaret, noticing a subdued irritation in his manner.

"The photograph brings out all the wonderful beauties of the architectural details;" he replied. "The sunlight only shows their present decay."

"'He that hath bent him o'er the dead,'"

began Rinaldo, speaking in English—

> "'Ere the first day of death has fled,
> Before decay's effacing fingers
> Have swept the lines where beauty lingers—'"

and he would have continued the quotation, but for D'Urbino's exclamation of surprise;

"I had no idea that you spoke English," he broke in; "and still less that you read Byron."

"Why not?" replied the polished *cameriere*.

"Yes; why not? as you say," retorted D'Urbino; "but I should hardly expect you to apply the whole quotation to the Venice of to-day,

"' 'Tis Greece, but living Greece no more.'

There is also this fault in the application; that death, when it seems lovely, is the work of a merciful providence, which destroys life out of the fulness of its love; while the decay of Venice is the consequence of a violent death, caused by the iron-hearted cruelty of man."

"We will not argue the question critically," replied the other. "There are two sides to the question, as I think you will admit."

"But there is only one side to the question as to whether my cousin is to obey my injunction to her to leave your interesting conversation, gentlemen;" interrupted Miss

Sandford, laying her hand on Margaret's arm. Mrs. Sandford, ever watchful and prudent, had noticed the increasing warmth of the conversation between the cavaliere and Rinaldo, and thought it well at once to recal her niece to her side. The two girls immediately walked away, and D'Urbino was about to follow them, when he was stopped by a half-whisper from Rinaldo.

"One moment's conversation with you," he said, returning to his native Italian. "But you must not seem to be talking secrets to me. Pretend to be looking at the jewels in my sword-hilt," he continued, taking hold of the sword, and offering it to D'Urbino's examination.

Too well practised in self-control to show any signs of surprise, D'Urbino instantly acted on the hint, and seemed to be absorbed in admiration of the gems and their setting.

"You were speaking English to Miss Osborne, before I came up," continued Rinaldo in the same low tone, while he seemed to be as busy in pointing out the beauties of his sword as D'Urbino was in inspecting them. The latter could scarcely repress a start of astonishment, but he replied at once :—

"How could you possibly know that? Surely you could not hear what we said?"

"No; I heard nothing," rejoined the other.

"You amaze me," said D'Urbino.

"I know it by the absence of your ordinary gesticulations, and the look of effort that was on your features. When you speak Italian, your gestures and looks are like those of other Italians. When you speak English, you unconsciously adopt the cold manner and look of the frigid Englishman."

"But how did you know until a few moments ago that I spoke English at all? Do you mean to say that you have been in the habit of comparing my Italian manner with my English manner? Are we really within the meshes of an accursed net such as this?"

"Others have studied your gifts of language, and I have benefited by their studies," rejoined Rinaldo. "But that you possessed English books, even if you did not speak English, it needed only this little volume to show. Control yourself, however, my friend, as you value your life, or at least your liberty."

As he spoke, he took from his pocket a small book, and handed it to D'Urbino, adding in a loud tone, so that everyone near them might hear—

"Suppose we take a turn in the fresh air; the heat is getting intolerable." Then in a whisper he added, "Now talk aloud about anything in the world you can think of."

The hint was understood, and to the gay crowd through whom they passed, it seemed that they were engaged in an animated antiquarian discussion, as to the date of certain buildings in Venice. Reaching the quadrangle—which is so characteristic a feature in the larger palaces of Rome, and which in this particular instance included a kind of arcade, or cloister, turning round three of its sides,—the two men at once sought the shelter and the shadow of the arched walk. A glance had shown Rinaldo the almost deadly paleness of his companion's face, though his step was firm, and his compressed lips and frowning brow revealed the intensity of the effort with which he restrained the passionate thoughts that were ready to burst out into words.

"You will ask how I possessed myself of this little book," said Rinaldo, speaking to D'Urbino's thoughts. "You will think me a thief as well as a——"

"Finish your sentence, in the name of all that is devilish," rejoined D'Urbino, as the other hesitated to utter the word which hung upon his lips.

"It is needless," replied the other, with perfect calmness. "Just now, the only question is as to my honesty. I found this book not a score of yards from where we are standing, not an hour ago. Pardon me, my friend, if I suggest that you are only a half-accomplished conspirator; if you drop the contents of your pockets in places where the first person who comes after you may be, not a friend, but——" and he paused again.

"You have of course opened the book, and looked it through," said D'Urbino, in a voice in which horror and anger seemed to be striving for the mastery.

"Including the various initials at the end, written in pencil," said his companion, completing his reply before the expected question was asked.

"And what course do you intend to take?" asked D'Urbino, with a bitterness almost savage in its intensity.

"None whatever," replied the other, "upon my honour."

"Honour!" echoed D'Urbino. "Is there

honour among——" and he in his turn cut short his sentence unfinished.

"As much as there is among conspirators," said Rinaldo. "Surely by this time you have learnt that it is possible, and even easy, to combine an enlightened love for revolutions with a still more enlightened love for one's own personal advancement."

"If all that is said is true," retorted D'Urbino, "you are now speaking from your own personal experience."

"I am," he rejoined, emphatically. "But yet it is possible to retain one's honour, even in such circumstances as those of which we are speaking."

"Possible—yes!" said D'Urbino; "but probable—no!"

"Yet there is a line which I think can be easily drawn between the honourable and the dishonourable, even in such circumstances as those we are hinting at."

"Is there?" asked D'Urbino; "I should be glad to know of its existence."

"You have heard every villainy attributed to me?" replied Rinaldo, as if asking a question.

"A good many, certainly," said his companion.

"Have I ever betrayed any man, acting on knowledge which I had obtained before—before I had the honour of a post in the household of the Holy Father?" he confidently retorted.

"I cannot say," said D'Urbino.

"Can you point to any single instance of such betrayal?"

"Honestly, then, I cannot," said the other.

"I thank you for the admission, such as it is," replied his companion.

"It is worth more than you imagine," said the other.

"If I were as black as you think me," answered Rinaldo, "I should not have returned you that book of English verses, at any rate with the pencillings at the end."

"You may have taken a copy of them, already, nevertheless," insinuated D'Urbino.

"I am a good-natured man, my young friend," replied the other, on the point of losing his self-control, "or your insinuations might have cost you dear. Do you not see that I have returned you the original, and that any mere copy would be worthless, so far as you are compromised? As to the initials themselves, they, and their full explanations have been communicated to the Government months ago."

"Oh! horrible, accursed, and hellish system!" exclaimed D'Urbino, in the bitterness of his soul.

"Most horrible and accursed!" exclaimed a voice, proceeding from a door which suddenly opened in the cloister wall as they passed, and was instantly shut again.

There was no mistaking the reality of the amazement which seized upon the two men alike.

"*Gran Dio!*" cried Rinaldo, "whose voice

was that? Is it possible that we have been overheard?"

"Hardly," rejoined D'Urbino; "yet why not? The door may have been opened just wide enough for any one inside to hear what we talked about without our noticing it in this dim light."

"You can scarcely suspect me of being in the plot?" asked Rinaldo.

"Circumstances are against you, nevertheless," retorted D'Urbino.

"They are, as I must admit; but I swear to you that I am as much amazed and bewildered as you are yourself," was Rinaldo's reply.

"Our only course at present is to return to the dancing rooms together," D'Urbino rejoined. And in a few moments they were again mixing with the brilliant throng upstairs.

Before the evening was over, D'Urbino once more found Rinaldo by his side.

"I have found out the truth," he said,

"as to the listener in the cloister. We were followed, when we went out, by one of the wild young *attachés* of the Embassy, on the look out for mischief; and of course they know all the rooms and back staircase of the house. It was all in jest that he waylaid us, and no harm will come of it. Only, for Heaven's sake, let it make you cautious how you talk politics out of doors in future."

CHAPTER III.

ESCAPED.

The following morning brought Henry Noel at a tolerably early hour to Mrs. Sandford's drawing-room, anxious, notwithstanding all his professional asceticism, to hear something of the preceding night's gaieties. To his surprise, he found that another visitor was already in full conversation with the three ladies. Della Porta was already cultivating their acquaintance with all practicable speed, and the party were deep in the discussion of the difference between English and Italian marriage customs.

"I am rejoiced to see you, Mr. Noel," said Margaret as soon as the ordinary salutations had been exchanged. "I am sure I shall find you on my side. Now, tell us at once, whether you do not in your heart condemn these continental ways."

"Absolutely, do you mean?" he asked, "or comparatively?"

"I don't understand you, I think," she replied.

"If you mean, do I think the foreign rule absolutely good in all respects? I must say no. But I think it on the whole at least as good as the prevailing English rule."

Amused at her cousin's blank look of disappointment, Helen came in to the rescue. "My dear Margaret," she cried, "how can you expect anything in the smallest degree enthusiastic from a man who is sworn to remain a bachelor all his days?"

"Not sworn," interposed Noel.

"What then?" asked Helen.

"Bound by a rule of the church," said he.

"Well," she rejoined, "it comes to the same thing in practice. It is a subject on

4—2

which you personally can have no knowledge whatsoever. You are brought up to the idea from your childhood, and it is as easy to you to put aside the notion of marrying, as if you were created without human feelings at all."

A fiery flush shot across the young priest's countenance, as Helen spoke, and his lips quivered with something very like anguish. Margaret saw it all in a moment, and came to his relief by turning the talk to a less hazardous aspect of the question.

"But, Marchese," she said, addressing Della Porta, "I should very much like to see how your Italian fashion of making a couple of generations live together, as one household, is made to work."

"Is it so difficult for you to understand?" he asked.

"With us," said Margaret, "it is quite a proverb that married sons should never live with their fathers and mothers. Mr. Noel will tell you that a mother-in-law, living in her married son's house, is the very type and pattern of everything that ruins the happiness of married life."

"But is not the unhappiness you speak of the natural result of your national passion for marrying for love?"

"I don't understand your reasoning," replied Margaret.

"What I mean is this," he went on; "that you English men and women marry with the expectation that you will be all in all to one another, and so wrapped up in conjugal bliss, that the presence of everybody else, even of your fathers and mothers, would be an intrusion and a restraint. Is it not so, Mrs. Sandford?" he continued, turning to Helen's mother.

"Not always, I think," replied the lady, who was honest enough in speaking the truth, though not much troubled with a painfully keen eye for logical inconsistencies.

"But generally so?" asked the pertinacious Marchese.

"Generally so, I allow," said Mrs. Sandford, "and, as I was just now saying, I am not so violent against your Italian ways as my niece is. She is still in the enthusiastic age."

"While I, who am just two years younger," broke in Helen, "am utterly and irremediably *blasée*, I suppose."

"It is my belief, Miss Sandford," said Noel, now recovering his equanimity, "that both men and women grow more tender as they grow older."

"Then you, at any rate, don't believe that I am hopelessly hardened just yet," asked Helen, with a mischievous look.

"How could I think so?" he replied, with a smile.

"But now to return to the subject of our Italian *ménage*," said Della Porta to Margaret, well aware that the conversation was assuming a tone held to be highly objectionable in the intercourse between the Italian clergy and laity; "you have seen little or nothing of our Italian domestic life, but you know a good deal of French life, which is based on the same principles as ours. You surely cannot adopt the vulgar idea that family ties are weaker in France than they are in England."

"I certainly think that the affection of husbands and wives is stronger among English people," Margaret replied.

"But taking life as a whole," he went on, "and considering that a married couple cannot cast off all thought for their fellow-creatures, would you say that the happiness of parents, of children, and of brothers and sisters, is less general on the English or on the French system?"

"Then you are in favour of men and women marrying just as their parents order them," broke in Helen, as impatient as she was illogical.

"Pardon me," rejoined Della Porta. "I think both the English and the French systems bad; but at the same time I see that there is good as well as evil in each of them. Another morning, if you will permit me, I should like to discuss the question more fully. To-morrow I am engaged, and for the rest of to-day also. May I call on you the day after?" and receiving the permission he desired, Della Porta took his leave.

"I suppose you guess at his engagement to-morrow?" observed Noel, when the door was closed. "To-morrow those two poor wretched men are to be executed."

The three ladies shuddered, and Margaret asked in wonder how Della Porta could be concerned in the bloody tragedy.

"Don't you know," said Noel, "that he is one of the *Confortatori*, whose duty it is to assist at these executions?"

"Another Roman mystery, I suppose," exclaimed Margaret. "Pray enlighten me, Mr. Noel," she continued. "There is really such an air of romance about all your proceedings here, that I don't wonder that we young Englishwomen find Rome the most delightful spot in the whole world,—at least, for one or two winters."

"The *Confortatori*," replied Noel, "are an institution of mediæval origin, and so ought to be specially interesting to us English people, with our love for anything that savours of a feudal origin."

"Such as Gog and Magog, I suppose," interposed Helen, "and the Lord Mayor's show, and the Royal Beef-eaters at Windsor. But pray don't look shocked at my levity, Margaret. These *Confortatori* have not the remotest resemblance to our notion of a London alderman, I assure you. Only conceive the Lord Mayor and Common Councilmen going about London disguised in big black cloaks, carrying lighted torches in their hands, and singing Psalms and Litanies!"

"What do you mean, Helen? And what makes you laugh, Mr. Noel, with all your attempts at looking severe?" asked Margaret.

"The *Confortatori*," rejoined he, "are a religious society, who assist criminals condemned to death, both while in prison and up to the last moment at the scaffold. The members are noble, or, as we might call them, of gentle birth; but it is only known to their friends that they belong to it, and their features are completely hidden when they appear in public."

"Yes," rejoined Margaret, in a bitter tone; "like nearly everything else here, where life is controlled either by the pious, the aristocratic, or the secret. These *Confortatori* seem to combine in themselves all these three elements of power. I don't wonder that my cousin laughs at them. And you yourself—surely you cannot like to see the principle of secrecy introduced into the practice of religion itself."

The vehemence and energy with which Margaret spoke restored the young priest to perfect seriousness in a moment. But he was in no humour for a discussion, and soon took his leave.

With an unacknowledged and trembling hope that some happy chance might enable them to catch a glimpse of the terrible *cortège* in which these mysterious *Confortatori* were to play a conspicuous part, the two cousins sallied forth for their usual walk betimes on the following morning, under the guardianship of Francesca Giorgione. With all their pretended dread of encountering the dreadful procession, Francesca was well aware that if by any accident they should be enabled to see it from a place of safety, they would in their hearts sincerely thank her for the mistake. After a little wandering from street to street, they found themselves compelled to take refuge from the rapidly increasing crowds in the house of a dealer in mosaic well known to Francesca's father. A few moments were enough to effect an arrangement for their taking possession of a large window commanding the whole length of a street along which the procession was to pass. Already the gathering excitement of the crowd gave token of its near approach.

"Look! look!" cried Francesca, her face quivering with emotion; "there they come—as far as ever your eyes can see!"

With a sickening feeling, totally unlike the passionate interest of Francesca, Margaret and her cousin stretched out their heads to the utmost. A picket of Papal dragoons was turning a corner, and slowly following the soldiery came a long procession of black vested figures, each of them carrying a blazing and smoking torch, while the sound of their gloomy funereal chantings gradually rose upon the air, in the occasional intervals between the harsh exclamations of the crowd, as it swayed to and fro, and made way for the dragoons. Immediately behind the *Confortatori* came an open carriage, or rather a large cart, bearing the two condemned criminals, and surrounded by a body of carbineers. Two priests were at the sides of the unhappy men, while a third held before them an image of the Virgin, and seemed by his gestures to be urging them to listen to his spiritual exhortations.

"There are two of them," said Helen to Francesca, as soon as she could recover herself after the first shock at the horrible sight.

"Yes—two, indeed!" replied Francesca, a gleam of indignation glancing from her eyes. "But only one who deserves to die."

"Why, what are their crimes?" asked Margaret, amazed.

"One of them is a parricide, and he ought to die. Look at him, signora! That is he, sitting, and in an agony of tears. He has not yet confessed, and the Padre is exhorting him."

As the procession drew near, the incidents of the awful scene almost explained themselves. The agitation of the crowd became wilder every moment. The women, of whom there were many, called aloud to the priests to tell them whether the men had confessed. Cries of "*Sono convertiti?*"—"Are they converted?" again and again struck the ears of the two cousins and their companion. The priests still shook their heads in reply. Just as the cart came within earshot, the cries of the women and of some few of the men in the crowd, became absolutely frantic. They raged against the obstinate criminals, reproaching them, and almost cursing them. "*Birboni!* will you die like Turks and heathens? You are going to be judged. Go! go!" they went on exclaiming in all the fury of the Italian temperament when roused to fever heat; "go! go! to be damned for ever!" Shortly afterwards, as the cart passed immediately beneath the window, the imprecations seemed to overcome the resistance of one of the two miserable men. He threw himself on his knees before the priest who was at his side, seized the crucifix with his hands, and passionately kissed it again and again. Cries of delight broke out from the crowd at the welcome sight, followed by renewed calls to his companion in misery to follow his example. All in vain, however. With a face from which all trace of colour had passed, the man remained unmoved alike by the earnest calls of the priests and the furious yellings of the mob. As the procession moved onwards, Francesca's passionate excitement gave place to a more quiet but even more intense emotion.

"He is innocent!" she whispered to Helen and Margaret.

"Gracious heavens!" cried Margaret; "is it possible? Perhaps a reprieve will come at the last moment."

"Never!" answered Francesca. "Donato's crime is one that *they* never forgive."

"But you said he was innocent of any crime?" asked Helen.

"His crime was committed against the priests, and that is a thing never forgiven. I will tell you more to-morrow." Then she suddenly broke out: "*Santa Vergine!* there is a rescue! Look forward, Signora, see!—see!—the soldiers are going to fire! There is a man cut down! there is another, and another!" But the shoutings and yellings of the crowd soon made Francesca's voice, all trembling with excitement, no longer intelligible; and Margaret and Helen could only guess at what was really taking place. It was clear that a deadly struggle was beginning between the soldiers and the crowd, which at the spot now reached by the procession, seemed almost entirely to consist of men. Forcing back the dense mass in front of them, the dragoons soon, however, cleared the way for the *Confortatori* and the condemned men to move onwards, and after proceeding a short distance farther on, the whole procession turned out of the street, through a large open gateway, and disappeared. The struggle between the troops and the crowd was here renewed with fresh fierceness, and Margaret, not yet familiar with the cries and gesticulations of an Italian mob, stood breathless with terror, expecting that nothing less than bloodshedding on a terrible scale must follow.

Meanwhile, the shouts and execrations of the populace were apparently dying away, when they suddenly burst forth with renewed vigour. The huge doors which had been forcibly closed when the procession passed through the gateway, were again thrown open, and the soldiers, the *Confortatori*, and the cart of the condemned, came forth in their original order, followed by some twenty or thirty men who had pushed themselves through, in company with the troops. As the cart itself emerged into the open street, a shout that seemed as if it must have been heard all over Rome, rent the air. Of the two condemned men one only remained. Everything else was unchanged, but the parricide alone was there. The intense interest of the mob seemed also to have subsided, and as soon as the streets were tolerably clear, the three women hastened homewards.

At the door of Mrs. Sandford's house the cousins encountered Henry Noel, looking the very picture of bewilderment, which quickly changed to an expression of very decided annoyance, when he learnt how they had been occupying themselves. To all their questionings about the escape of the condemned man, he would only reply that the rescue was utterly inexplicable. He had himself spoken to the officers in command of the dragoons and the carbineers, who had asserted that the criminal had vanished before their eyes. "All Rome," he added, "will be in an uproar. The police will be at work before an hour is passed. But I know the place where the escape was effected, as well as any spot in the world, and I assure you that it is physically impossible that the man could have got away unperceived. To-morrow I will come and tell you all."

And with this promise the two cousins were forced, very unwillingly, to content themselves.

CHAPTER IV.

MORNING VISITORS.

"Well! what is the news?" was Helen's eager question to Noel, as soon as the morning salutations were over when he came to fulfil his promise.

"Absolutely none," he replied, "except that the whole thing is utterly inexplicable, and we are all as much in the dark as ever. In no possible way can we account for Donato's disappearance."

"Do you mean that there is positively no outlet from the quadrangle, or whatever it is, from which he made his escape?" asked Margaret.

"None whatever," he said. "The place itself is a very large square, surrounded by a disused cloister, once belonging to a convent long since suppressed. Nobody could by any possibility scale the walls, and the gates by which the procession entered were shut the whole time it was inside the inclosure."

"But what business had the procession there at all?" asked Margaret.

"There is an old image of the Madonna, still remaining in a recess inside the cloister, towards which the people have a great devotion; and it is not uncommon for condemned criminals to be taken there on the way to execution, as on this occasion."

"One of your Roman superstitions, I suppose," observed Margaret. "Of course, Mr. Noel, you don't believe in the special efficacy of prayers made in one place rather than another?"

"It is a dangerous thing to disturb popular beliefs," he replied.

"Doubtless," said Margaret. "But is it not often equally dangerous to encourage them?"

"Come, come," interposed Helen; "reserve your controversies till we have heard the story to an end. Is there no door, or other concealed opening by which the man may have got away?"

"None, whatsoever," said Noel; "every nook and cranny has been searched again and again, and not a trace of such a thing has been found."

"Nor any trap-door opening into a cellar, or underground passage?"

"Nothing of the kind."

"And no dark recesses, or half blocked-up niches, in which the man may have effectually dodged the soldiers and the other officials?"

"No; such a thing would have been impracticable. There are one or two places where a man might have hidden himself for a minute or so, but not longer. Then, too, nobody seems to have seen Donato jump down from the cart where he was placed."

"Is that absolutely the fact?" inquired Margaret.

"Absolutely. I have myself questioned the priests who were by his side, as closely as I could; and they most positively declare that the man was gone without their perceiving it. The confusion was tremendous, it is true; but there were none but soldiers and *Confortatori* near them. In fact some of the *Confortatori* clambered up the cart, and held the two criminals fast to prevent their escape."

"How many of the mob had rushed in before the gates were shut?—perhaps they had a hand in the matter," pursued Margaret.

"Some twenty or thirty, perhaps," he rejoined; "but that was nothing to the purpose. The great fact remains, that when the procession was reformed, in order to leave the quadrangle, Donato could not be found. It was simply impossible that he could be hidden anywhere; and everyone of the crowd that had forced itself in, was closely scrutinised before he was allowed to pass out."

"And you have no clue of any kind to the mystery?"

"None."

"And what do the police and the magistrates, and the rest of the world say to it all?"

"You will laugh, Miss Osborne, I know very well, when I tell you. There are two opinions running like wildfire through Rome, by way of solving the mystery. Some will have it that Donato was carried off by the devil, and others that he was miraculously saved by *Santa Maria dei fiori*, as the image in the cloister is commonly called."

At this announcement Mrs. Sandford looked shocked, her daughter laughed outright, and Margaret's lips quivered with amusement.

"It is no laughing matter, I assure you," continued Noel; "you can have no idea of the mischief that is done when these notions get hold of our Romans, both men and women. We may possibly be on the eve of a frantic outbreak. The old story of the winking virgin is already revived."

"And yet you enlightened gentlemen have not the courage to put a stop to the preposterous follies which you yourselves totally disbelieve."

"Pardon me, Miss Osborne," Noel replied; "if I say that you seem to be the most unbelieving woman alive. But let me entreat you to be careful in what you say while you are here. The air is filled with reports about the countenance we English people give to the revolutionary party already."

"I am glad to hear you say *we* English," said Margaret. "But how about the miraculous winking? Is it the image in the cloister that winked? and who first saw the winking?"

"That is the worst thing in the whole matter," rejoined Noel. "This very morning I met that dangerous and clever young fellow, the sculptor D'Urbino, and I taxed him with what I had heard of his going about among the Trasteverini and elsewhere, and spreading the story about the winking; declaring, too, that he himself distinctly saw the miracle with his own eyes."

"Well, and what did he say? Do you know that we made the acquaintance of this terrible gentleman at the ball the other night?"

Noel's countenance fell, as he replied, "I am aware that you did."

"And who in heaven's name, told you this?" cried Margaret, angrily. "Are you one of an association for spying out the ways and words of your acquaintances? Surely, Mr. Noel, you will admit, as a gentleman, that for you, being a priest, to busy yourself with ball-room tittle tattle about us, verges very nearly upon the impertinent."

"The information was given me without my asking for it," retorted Noel, with a violent effort at self-restraint.

"May we ask who was your informant?" inquired Helen.

"I am sorry not to be able to tell you," said Noel.

"In other words, you will not," retorted Helen, now thoroughly piqued.

"Or rather," struck in Margaret, "you dare not."

"Margaret! Helen!" exclaimed Mrs. Sandford, breaking her wonted silence; "surely you are forgetting what is due to Mr. Noel."

"Pray say nothing about it, Mrs. Sandford," he replied. "I must confess to have deserved a rebuke, though perhaps a less severe one. But we are all here in a difficult position, and I must entreat for a charitable interpretation of what I said."

He spoke with such unaffected sincerity and modesty, that Helen and Margaret were at once appeased, and Margaret continued the conversation in a friendly tone.

"But about this same supposed miracle," she said; "is it stated that it took place while the escape of the criminal was being effected?"

"So I understood D'Urbino to say," replied Noel.

"Of course he does not pretend to believe in the story he is spreading."

"Not for an instant. That is the worst of the matter, as I said just now. He and other well known Liberals are propagating the story, to work upon the superstition of the mob, and make them believe that the scoundrel Donato is under the special protection of heaven."

"Yes, I see it all plainly enough," replied Margaret; "and you also see, I trust, that superstitious feelings may be worked upon on both sides of the question."

"And who is this villain Donato," interposed Helen, "whom you and all the authorities seem to detest so heartily? What is his crime?"

"He was quarrelling with a disreputable priest in a house at Tivoli, and in the heat of passion struck him in the face. The priest fell backwards with his head upon the stone floor, was picked up almost insensible, fell into a fever, and soon died."

"And for this accident in a trumpery brawl," exclaimed Margaret, "the man was to have been executed. *I* should call the execution a judicial murder."

"It is a painful story," he replied, sadly enough. "You are aware that as the priesthood are forbidden to use violence themselves, they are protected by the severest penalties against those who attack them."

"But where is the proof that this Donato did anything more than occurs in nine out of ten of your Roman quarrels?"

"The judge who tried him decided that there was an intent to kill."

"But what said the jury?"

"There are no juries in Rome," replied Noel, sadly as well as gravely.

"Then I must say that if the Madonna did wink in order to set Donato free, she showed a vast deal more good sense than miraculous images in general are in the habit of showing. You may put me down," she went on, undeterred by Noel's evident annoyance, "on the list of those who hold to the truth of the winking story. If the image did not wink, it ought to have winked; and for once we will believe that a hideously ugly image did its duty. By the way," she continued, "I suppose it *is* a hideous image."

"I have seen uglier," replied Noel, in his secret heart thinking Margaret as flippant in manner as he felt her to be unanswerable in the way of argument. It was a relief to him, at the moment, to hear Della Porta announced, and immediately afterwards to see the Marchese himself enter the room. The subject would now, he thought, be dropped; but at any rate, he was sure of Della Porta's support in making the best case possible in favour of anything that was Italian. He soon found that the discussion must be continued.

"I was on the point of putting a very important question," Margaret began, "to our friend here, but he is so terribly cautious, that I suspect I should have got no satisfactory reply. How is it that all these popular and miraculous images are invariably abominations in the way of ugliness? Here is my cousin Helen, who has confessed to me that they generally remind her of the black dolls that hang up in front of the rag-and-bottle shops in our English towns."

Noel only winced, but Della Porta smiled and replied,

"I don't quite see to what your question points, Miss Osborne."

"What I mean is this," she continued, "that I cannot reconcile this universal preference for hideousness in the objects of their veneration with the undoubted fondness for art, in some shape or other, with which the Italian people are credited."

"It is a curious and puzzling question," said Della Porta, "setting aside the religious aspect of the subject. I hardly know how to answer you, but I suspect that the explanation is to be found in that intensity and vehemence of passion which I suppose is characteristic of all Italians, saving the cooler Piedmontese. The ignorant multitude is, of course, not very critical in its notions of the beautiful; and I fancy that the heat of their pious feelings suffuses every object of their regard with a sort of haze of light and colour, which transforms even Miss Sandford's black doll into an attractive statuette."

"I understand what you mean," rejoined Margaret, "though I don't see its force."

"Well now," continued Della Porta, "surely you don't suppose that an affectionate mother sees ugliness in her children to the same extent that other people see it."

"True enough," said Margaret, "but you cannot compare a mother's feelings towards her children with the fondness of these people for what, after all, is simply a wooden doll."

"I think you underrate the intensity of the devout feelings of our people," replied Della Porta. "It is not a question as to the reality and depth of their religious principles, but rather as to their emotional sensitiveness. You English people are cool, even where the judgment is fully convinced. But in our Italian peasantry and labouring town people a passionate vehemence of feeling is a natural result of the convictions of the judgment."

"You mean," suggested Margaret, "that being brought up to regard these images as possibly miraculous, they are predisposed to overlook their substantial ugliness."

"You could not have put it better," said the Marchese, with the courtly grace which seemed natural to him. "Observe, however," he continued, "that I am not for an instant defending the tone of teaching you speak of. What I am anxious is that you should judge us from the Italian point of view, and not from the English."

"That is exactly what I always say to her about marriage customs," broke in Helen, who cared not a straw for the image difficulty.

"About these same marriage customs, then," said Margaret; "how can you possibly account for the adoption of your Italian system by this very impulsiveness and passionateness which so much affect your religious proceedings?"

"Really I do not see the difficulty," replied Della Porta, with a most evident increase of interest in the discussion. "It is this very impulsiveness and passionateness which drives us to our national habits in the matter. I am convinced that if we arranged our marriages on your English notion that 'Love shall still be lord of all'—you see I read English poets nevertheless—the whole fabric of society would be broken up."

"Yet I have surely heard you condemn your system as miserable," exclaimed Helen.

"Not altogether, I am confident," said Della Porta, "but only its frequent abuses. And with all its abuses, the opposite system would be ten times as disastrous. It is difficult to explain to you what a frenzy is the passion of love with most of our hot-blooded race."

"But why is it necessarily a passion at all?" asked Margaret. "It is very seldom anything of the kind among English people, except in novels."

"That is exactly where the differences of national temperament show themselves," rejoined Della Porta, while Helen and Noel felt the discussion growing almost painful in interest.

"It is just because the feeling, or whatever you may call it, of love is almost certain to become a flaming, burning passion in the Italian heart, that our marriage arrangements are so necessary. They talk of the '*furia Francese*' in matters of fighting, but they might quite as well talk of the '*furia Italiana*' in matters of love making."

"Tell me, then, further," asked Margaret, "do you find, as a matter of fact, that this '*furia Italiana*' always comes after marriage and that a young couple who begin life on the system of a limited liability partnership like a firm of bankers or merchants, gradually become the most devoted of lovers after the true Phyllis and Corydon type?"

"You mis-state the theory, as well as the practice and its results," he replied. "It is because marriage is not a partnership on a limited liability basis, that we enter upon it with a very tolerable expectation that it will prove successful. When the whole of a man's existence depends upon the manner in which he fulfils the duties of his partnership, he is naturally disposed to make the best of his opportunities."

"But suppose your happy couple find out that they are personally odious to one another before the honeymoon is fairly over?"

"There again," Della Porta replied, "your very phrase indicates a want of appreciation of our system. We look for no honeymoon of enraptured bliss, to be followed by a rapid disenchantment."

"But why assume a disenchantment at all?"

"I do not assume it." It is the very term 'honeymoon' that implies it. And what I was going to say is this; that a couple who do not begin their married life with the recognition of the fact that they are certain to find themselves at issue in sundry matters, at once set about making the best of everything."

"Their bliss is rare," interposed Noel,

"but their disappointments are rarer still;" and he at once felt supremely uncomfortable at having ventured into the very non-clerical subject.

"Bravo!" exclaimed Della Porta, with a laugh. "I cannot add *experto crede*, Noel; but the most philosophical of epigrammatists could not have put it better."

Noel, however, being of opinion that he had already said too much, took the first opportunity of bringing his visit to an end, and was speedily followed by the Marchese.

"Well?" cried Helen, when the two gentlemen were fairly gone, with a significant look at her cousin.

"Well?" echoed Margaret, with another smile equally significant, but showing more surprise.

"Are we not on the eve of a most interesting announcement; or rather, I suppose, I ought to say, a most interesting negociation?" Helen asked.

"I have not the faintest conception of your meaning," rejoined Margaret.

"Is it really that you don't understand me, or is your ignorance only affectation," asked her cousin.

"I assure you I am utterly in the dark," rejoined Margaret.

"Surely you see that the courtly Marchese has something in view," said Helen. "At any rate, you will never have to be ashamed of a husband's ill-breeding. His manner is absolutely perfect."

"And you really believe that I am the lode-star that attracts him?" asked Margaret. "Are you serious in what you say?"

"Never more serious in my whole life. Why should he try so hard to convince you of the charms of Italian matrimony, except with an object before him?"

"With *an* object before him, I grant you. But I am not the object he is aiming at, rest assured, my dear. I don't pretend to understand the ways of Italian lovers, but of this I am convinced, that no thought of love-making to me has ever entered the Marchese's head for a single moment."

Helen was still unconvinced; and a pleasant suspicion was rising in her thoughts, which she took no pains to crush. For the rest of the morning she sat at the open window, with her eyes upon the moving life below, but her thoughts in a cloud-land, not the less captivating in its beauty, because its outlines were vague and ever changing, and its dim vistas melted away into a distance, where no forms were defined and all was grey and sober in tone.

CHAPTER V.

D'URBINO IN HIS STUDIO.

THE studio of Cavaliere D'Urbino, in the Via Felice, was much like other sculptors' studios, except in its somewhat unusual neatness, cleanliness, and absence of affectation. Studios, whether of sculptors or painters, are of various kinds, and the curious in such matters are apt to discover in their contents and condition distinct evidences of the personal characters of their owners.

Some look as if they were arranged with a sole eye to business, and as if the painter or sculptor who wrought in them was infinitely superior to the surroundings amidst which he wielded the brush or modelled the clay. In others the occupier seems to find it essential to the freedom of his thought and the activity of his hands that nothing should strike his eyes that could suggest the mean, or sordid, or prosaic realities of common life. Others are finical and dandyish in their furniture and in the disposition of the ornaments which their owners find to be soothing to their feelings and pleasing to their self-love. Others again are flagrantly theatrical, and display a crowd of artistic objects, including a careful selection from the works of the artist who thus vicariously exhibits himself, and so to say, attitudinises for the benefit of his friends and visitors. Then, further, there is the studio which tells only too well that he who lives in it is a manufacturer of works on canvas, or in marble, in which the costume and accessories are everything that is correct, and the only thing that is wanting is the movement and expression of human life itself. This latter class of picture and sculpture factories is less common in Rome than it is in London, the Eternal City not possessing those vast annual exhibitions of paintings which in England serve to show the vast wealth of purchasers, and the spirited competition which exists among artists eager for their applause, or rather for the contents of their purses.

Among the simpler sort of studios D'Urbino's was conspicuous for its methodical and business-like arrangements. But for the presence of some plaster casts, two or three busts and figures in marble, none of them completely finished, and the usual apparatus for modelling in clay, it might have passed for a half-furnished dining room or saloon. Three days after the affair of the execution and the escape of Donato, its owner was standing before a nearly finished female head in clay, and examining it under every variety of light. It was slightly colossal in size, and though evidently a portrait, exhibited that wild, dreamy, and at the same time suffering look which is rarely seen even in the most expressive of living faces. D'Urbino was still scrutinising the result of his labours, when an elderly-looking woman opened the door of the room, and walked unceremoniously towards him.

"Here is that girl coming again, Signore," she exclaimed, "it's really scandalous. I wonder she can have the face to do it, and you to encourage her, and Signora Bianca now married and gone into the country to live, and me too busy to look after your doings; and you know it's against all the commands of the Holy Father, and I wonder how her own father can allow her goings on, and it's—" and here she fairly stopped in her vehement harangue, for want of breath.

"Go on, my dear Bettinella, pray," said D'Urbino, in a mocking but good-natured way; "you must have at least a hundred more reasons to prove that poor Francesca is very wicked, for coming here, and I am very wicked for asking her to come."

"I am not Bettinella," retorted the old woman, now no longer panting; "my name is Elisabetta, and you only call me wrong in order to flatter me into holding my tongue."

"Well, then, Bettone, or Bettinaccia—will that suit you, if you don't like such a pretty name as Bettinella? As for Elisabetta, it's out of the question. I don't believe you were ever christened such a name."

"Nonsense, Signore," said the still exasperated Elisabetta, or Betta, as she was addressed by everybody except her young master, one of whose favourite amusements was to tease her, by applying to her an endless succession of those diminutives and other perversions of proper names, to which the Italian language so readily lends itself.

"There she is, at the door!" she cried; "am I to let her in, or am I not?"

"Betta! Betta!" said the sculptor, "allow

me to tell you that you talk like an idiot, and not like the sensible woman you really are. You know perfectly well that Francesca comes here for no purpose but to sit as my model."

"I know nothing of the kind," she retorted. "There! there she is knocking again! — am I to let her in, or am I not?"

"If you don't let her in, I know what will happen."

"What will happen? Will she go away affronted, and never come here any more?"

"By no means. Guess again," said he, in a still more aggravating manner.

"Signor D'Urbino, I will leave your service this very day, if you go on tormenting and insulting me in this cruel way."

"By all means, Betta," he replied, "only in the mean time, do me the favour to open the door to Francesca, or else——"

"Yes? or else?"

"Or else I shall be obliged to go and let her in myself."

Upon this she flung herself out of the room, admitted the unconscious object of her objurgations, showed her into the studio, then disappeared, discomfited. If she had remained, she would have seen the young sculptor advance to meet Francesca, and greet her with a business-like cordiality that showed that his account of the purpose of her visits was nothing more nor less than the simple truth. Francesca was soon placed in the proper position and under the proper light for the progress of the modelling.

As she sat down, evidently with no disposition for conversation, D'Urbino thought that he had never before seen the very expression that he wished to communicate to the lifeless clay so vividly present in the living countenance before him. The wildness and the dreaminess that he sought to express, were often to be seen overspreading

Francesca's handsome features. The bantering, teasing talk in which he was wont to indulge during her frequent sittings, seemed naturally to arouse in her mind some strange sort of irritation, more serious than he could account for from his knowledge of the girl and of her circumstances; and at times her eyes gleamed with that brilliancy which it is so difficult to embody, either in marble or on canvas, without melodramatic exaggeration. Then, apparently from no external cause, the latent passion would usually give place to a softer mood, the full dark eyes would fasten themselves without effort upon some unseen sight that held her in its charm; and again and again D'Urbino felt that if he could only fix in the obedient clay the look of the girl's face, during the few moments when the gleaming brightness melted into the tender gaze of the spell-bound dreamer, the grand aim of his ambition would be more than half accomplished.

But it was just at such moments, that with all his profound love for the sculptor's art, he felt its chief deficiency. As to the popular theory about the chilling effects of the want of colour in a marble statue, otherwise transcending the noblest works of the painter's skill, he knew too well that it is little more than the excuse of the mere academic practitioner. It was only when he spent hours and days in the vain attempt to give a real vitality to the eyes of his busts, that he felt his hand paralysed, and he was tempted to dash his modelling tools or his mallet and chisel on the floor.

So far as the movements of the brow, the eyelids and the pose of the head could supply suggestions for achieving the success he longed for, Francesca was a model among ten thousand. The features of Roman women are often cast in that almost superb and slightly sensuous mould, which the sculptor most loves when he attempts the heroic or the ideal. But their brains are not of the same lofty stamp as their countenances. Their emotions are as soft, as passionate, and as intense, as the eyes and lips which express them are beautiful. But whether from natural character, or from the shallowness of their own education and that of their daily companions, both men and women, it is rarely that they show any indications of an intelligence either keen or profound.

That Francesca was really one of these rare exceptions to the ordinary rule, D'Urbino had long been convinced. In fact, it was from having accidentally detected signs of this depth in her nature, that he had made acquaintance with her father and with herself, with a view to engaging her as his model. And it was through a little adroit eulogy of these gifts that he had persuaded the mosaic worker to allow her to attend at his studio, but even then only with the express stipulation that his sister, the Signora Bianca, should always be present at the sittings.

At first the stipulation was rigidly complied with, but the illness of a friend had first called Bianca away from Rome, and after that came her own marriage; and but for certain unknown political ties between the sculptor and the humbler artist, Francesca would certainly have been forbidden to pay any more of those visits which so scandalised the suspicious Elisabetta. What was the exact nature of those ties Francesca herself knew not, though she drew her own conclusions as to the mysterious character of an intimacy, which, though not of a very long date, had created in her father's mind the most undoubting confidence in the Cavaliere's truth and honour.

To-day it seemed to D'Urbino that Francesca was about to prove herself a model, possessing every quality that he could desire. She had not sat ten minutes before him, while he was carefully giving what he expected would be the last finishing touches to the contour of the lips, when he was made unpleasantly conscious that his work must have been hitherto very feeble and blundering, so marked were the corrections it seemed to need.

Then, looking up stedfastly at the girl's face, taken as a whole, he suddenly saw that in its expression there was an element which he had never before discerned. In the mouth, which he fancied he had so clumsily failed to copy, he now detected that very intensity of sadness and suffering which he had long laboured to communicate to his work. A thrill shot through his susceptible nature, partly of mere artistic hope and gratification, partly of increased interest in a character which had hitherto suggested nothing more absorbing than materials for critical study.

With slow and careful touches he at once set about correcting his previous work, and for some time not a word escaped his lips or those of Francesca herself. At length, with a heavy sigh, her unwonted mood passed away, and she seemed to wake to the realities of the living world around her. With the change in Francesca's mood, D'Urbino's mood changed also, and he could not resist that tendency to teasing and bantering which he seldom had under control.

"We are both of us very grave to-day, Francesca," he began. "Was it the sight of the fight between the soldiers and the crowd that so depressed your spirits that you have not had a word to say this morning?"

"How do you know that I saw the fight at all?" she replied.

"I was told so by some friends of mine, and yours also," said D'Urbino.

"I did not know that we had any friends common to us both," she rejoined, with an evident touch of bitterness in the thought.

"A week or two ago we had not, it is true," he said; "but now the circle of my friends, or at least of my acquaintances, is enlarged. It has been whispered to me that you saw the sight in company with two very captivating young English ladies."

A flush of surprise overspread Francesca's whole face for a moment, as she replied: "I did not know they were your friends, Signore."

"Then I am sure your conversation with them did not turn upon myself, which is not flattering to my vanity, Francesca."

"Why should it have turned upon Cavaliere D'Urbino, more than upon any other gentleman in Rome?" asked Francesca.

"Solely because I had the honour of dancing with both those charming English women at the French Embassy, a few nights ago," said he.

"I suppose the subject would have been thought not fit for talking over, with a poor mosaic-worker's daughter," rejoined Francesca, with a sharpness of tone that provoked him to tease her still more.

"My dear Francesca," he said, "you are

hardly recovered from your late illness, and do not view the affairs of human life with your usual placid indifference. Nothing, I assure you, can be more amiable than the two ladies in question."

"Of course you have cultivated their acquaintance carefully," suggested Francesca.

"I will take you into my confidence," he rejoined, in the half serious, half joking way which he loved, and which Francesca abhorred. "I made an excuse about showing them some Venetian pictures, and have found them even more charming in their own home than in the splendours of the ball."

"I do not doubt it," replied Francesca, curtly.

"Were it not that my heart is already given away to my marble handiworks," he rejoined, "I assure you that I should fly from the society of these English, unless I wished my peace of mind to be destroyed for ever."

"I never heard of a man falling in love with a statue," she replied.

"That only shows that you were not properly instructed in ancient mythology in the days of your youth, Francesca," he rejoined, perfectly well aware that if there was any one thing especially distressing to the poor girl, it was any allusion to her defective education. In her vexation she started from her position, and her long hair, which had been knotted up so as to satisfy the sculptor's exacting taste, fell loose upon her shoulders. Almost in tears with pain and annoyance, she quickly re-arranged it, and entreated D'Urbino to tease her no more, with a simple humility of manner which puzzled him. But the folds and masses of the hair were not what they had been before, and after offering her many unsuccessful suggestions, D'Urbino laid aside his working tools, and tried with one or two gentle touches of his own, to re-arrange the beautiful but refractory coils according to his wishes.

Nothing could be more respectful or delicate than his handling of the superb locks, but he was surprised to find that Francesca trembled violently, and when one of his hands slipped and for a moment rested upon her forehead, her self-control gave way and she burst into an agony of tears. The hour for Elisabetta to come in with his usual midday meal was close at hand, and D'Urbino felt half wild, as he thought of the awkwardness of the situation if she should find Francesca in her present condition. Happily he was a man of rapid thought, and with a word to Francesca, saying that he would go and desire his servant to bring a draught of water to refresh her, he hastily left the room. The Cavaliere's knowledge of women was not very profound, but he made a shrewd guess that if anything would tend to stop Francesca's tears, it would be the fear of being discovered by the disagreeable Elisabetta in so unpleasant a condition. The draught of water was of course a fiction, as his real intention was to keep Elisabetta out of the studio altogether. The plan was successful, and when he returned after a short absence, Francesca had regained her composure, and the sitting ended happily.

CHAPTER VI.

THE GATHERING IN THE COLISEUM.

"Betta! Betta! Bettina? Bettinaccia! Bettinaccianella! Bettinella mia! Elisabetta! *Mille diavole!* is the woman gone deaf, or run away, that she keeps me here shouting myself hoarse?"

So shouted and grumbled the Cavaliere as soon as Francesca was fairly out of the house.

"Oh! here you are at last," he added, as the old woman made her appearance, bearing a tray on which was set out the hungry sculptor's midday refreshment.

"Are you aware, Betta mia," he remarked, as she placed it upon a table near him, "that it is at the least half an hour after the time you are bound under the severest penalties to have my modest meal prepared for me? Why, what is this?" he continued, missing the cutlets that were to form the substantial portion of the repast. "Salad! bread! dried figs! Do you take me for a Trappist, Betta? and what is this in the basin? Soup? yes; well; this is not what I ordered. Do you wish to starve me, or poison me before my time?"

"Patience, Eccellenza!" replied the old woman, in a propitiatory tone, and using the humble term of respect which she always adopted when she wished to mollify her master.

"I had the misfortune to spoil the cutlets, but the soup is excellent, and will abundantly satisfy your appetite."

"Bah!" cried the Cavaliere, after tasting the subject of the eulogy, "what in the name of all that is detestable have you compounded here, you faithless woman?"

"The soup is surely admirable, Eccellenza," she persisted, "though it is not flavoured with the flesh meat which the Church forbids on Fridays; and this is Friday, Signore."

"Confound the Church!" D'Urbino was on the point of exclaiming aloud, but he kept the anathema to himself, only warning the contumacious Betta to beware how she trifled with him any more in the matter of his eating, as he betook himself to his uninviting meal, while the self-constituted guardian of his morals made haste to relieve him of her presence. But what would have been his wrath if he had followed her to her own domain, and there beheld the missing cutlets reposing uncooked in a corner of the kitchen?

"Ah!" she was saying to herself, with a grin of satisfaction, as her eyes rested on the dish where the forbidden meat was lying; "I will keep him from one wickedness, at any rate. He shall have no flesh meat on

Fridays, if I tell ten thousand lies to prevent it. The cutlets will do very well to-morrow instead; and he may thank me for the one good deed he has done to-day."

Such were Betta's morals, and if they were somewhat loose in the matter of truth-telling, and her views on vicarious virtue were scarcely to be justified by any casuistry that is to be found written by reverend hands, are they much worse or more hazy than those which prevail in the most Protestant kitchens of England? Betta's standard of right and wrong was framed upon the purely ecclesiastical model; and she was surely no worse than the orthodox lady's-maid who would not for the world make free with her mistress's purse, but has no scruple in making free with her dresses by wearing them whenever no malicious informer can report upon her rogueries. And was the chuckle with which Betta congratulated herself whenever she could cheat her master into an unwilling conformity with sacerdotal rules, much less rational than the satisfaction of those teachers of our own who persuade their followers that they have become models of piety by the substitution of the dissipations of the platform for the dissipations of the playhouse?

If Betta had lived in London she would doubtless have been a devoted attendant on every possible occasion when the orators of the platform discourse on the spiritual destitution of far-off heathens, or the hopeless condition of Irish Papists. As, however, her lot was cast in Rome, she found her spiritual emotions sufficiently excited by taking a part in the proceedings of all the pious confraternities which were within her reach. The begging *Sacconi*, with all the mysterious rumours that were afloat as to their high rank in the social and ecclesiastical world, had a special attraction for her vulgar mind. She herself could bestow on them only very small contributions, but what she did give she gave with an exquisite zest as she reflected that the disguised mendicants were perhaps the owners of the most magnificent palaces in Rome, or even princes of the Church themselves.

Such being her ordinary feelings, it was with a peculiar sense of refreshment and self-complacency that she perceived a pair of these religious maskers approaching, as she stood lounging at the house door just after her exploit for the forcible conversion of the recalcitrant D'Urbino. According to their wont, they walked on different sides of the street, and Betta's hand was speedily thrust into her enormous pocket in search of the bajoccho which she intended to be her offering. Accordingly, it was dropped into the mendicant's bag the moment that he came up to her; but to her surprise, instead of immediately returning to her the customary reverence, he held out to her a letter, and requested her in a subdued voice to take it to her master without delay, adding some sort of vague threat of spiritual mischiefs that would afflict her, if she ventured on disobedience or betrayed the source whence the letter came. Such an unprecedented proceeding on the part of a *Saccone*, who she had heard was always under a vow of silence during his quest, was quite sufficiently startling, apart from the awful words with which her compliance was enforced. There was nothing for it, however, but to obey, and that instantly.

"Who gave you this note?" exclaimed D'Urbino, the moment he had glanced at its contents.

"It was given to me by a stranger," said Betta, noting well the look of amazement with which D'Urbino read the communication.

"Did he tell you it was for me? There is no address upon it," continued D'Urbino.

"He desired me to bring it instantly to you," she replied, but to every further question of the bewildered sculptor she opposed a resolute silence, and D'Urbino at last made up his mind to say no more, and at once dismissed her.

The letter was as follows:—

"Carry nothing about with you that may excite suspicion or compromise any one, and leave nothing in your rooms that you do not wish all the world to see." This was all. There was no signature, and the handwriting gave not the slightest clue to its authorship. Was it a hoax, or the warning of a friend? And if the latter, how could a friend be in the secret of the danger which the warning evidently implied to be approaching? It is one of the many evils of a despotic government, and especially of a clerical government, which is of necessity despotic because it is irresponsible, that while suspicion permeates the whole fabric of society, it is almost impossible to trace any rumour to its real source, and few people can thoroughly trust even their dearest friends or their daily associates.

However, it could do D'Urbino no harm

to act upon the hints he had received; and the more so as he was on the point of starting for the Coliseum, where a popular preaching friar was to discourse on the guilt of believing that the escaped convict Donato had been liberated by any heavenly aid. It was expected that the announcement would bring an enormous gathering of the poor to hear their favourite orator, even though he might take a view of his subject to which many of them were vehemently opposed. At the same time, though it was easy enough for D'Urbino to carry about with him no compromising papers, it was not a little difficult to extemporise a place of concealment at home for sundry suspicious letters, papers, and books, where no acuteness or violence of police agents could find them.

After much fruitless pondering, D'Urbino hit upon a plan that seemed to promise well. Taking down the few hollow plaster busts that were ranged upon a shelf against the wall, he deposited within their cavities the letters and documents which he wished to conceal, and then proceeded to fill up the openings with plaster of Paris, so that the casts would appear to be solid throughout, the weight of the real contents giving colour to the idea. What with the selection of the compromising papers, the stowing them away in their fragile receptacles, and the preparing of the plaster for closing them safely in, so much time was occupied, that when D'Urbino reached the Coliseum he found the preacher already at his post, and a vast audience listening to his fiery eloquence.

The crowd was so dense that it was with no little difficulty that D'Urbino forced his way to a spot where he could hear the speaker's voice, and even then it was nearly impossible to catch every word that he uttered, through the mutterings and exclamations which occasionally broke from the audience, as they were either delighted or irritated with what they heard. Immediately around the platform on which the preacher stood were gathered a body of police agents, sufficiently strong to protect him from violence, in case the agitation should culminate in an actual riot.

Conscious of the protection, and being really a man of iron nerve himself, the Capuchin grew bolder and bolder as he saw that his oratory was telling upon his excitable hearers. As a matter of argument, the sermon was worthless, but its rhetoric was in the highest degree ingenious. He assumed, without even pretending to prove it, that the cause of the priesthood was the cause of God, and that whosoever injured a priest, even of humblest class, was in reality striking a blow at Jesus Christ himself. Then suddenly, with wonderful dramatic power, he described the various incidents in the Gospel narrative of the Passion, filling up the Biblical outline; and even changing his voice and gestures as he repeated the words of the several characters of the history.

At last, having stirred up the feelings of his audience to fever heat, making many of the women and some few of the men sob and shed tears, as he dwelt on the insults and the violence offered to the Sacred Person, whose sufferings he was recounting, he slowly uttered the name of the escaped criminal, and introduced him as having been in spirit among the foremost blasphemers and murderers in Jerusalem. Then, turning to the tall crucifix which was fixed by his side, upon the platform, he addressed to it one of those daring invocations which are in favour with Italian preachers of a certain class, but of whose effect it is impossible to give any real idea by description.

It was in substance a pathetic lamentation that the wickedness of man could be so malignant as to offer violence to that which is divine.

During this portion of the sermon the

profoundest silence reigned around the preacher, and so far his oratory was a grand practical success. But like many another speaker, he knew not when to stop. The moment his invocation was ended, he turned round to the audience and asked them with bitter scorn whether it was possible that a miracle could be worked on behalf of a wretched criminal who could be guilty of such awful wickedness. Heaping relentless ridicule upon the report of the interference of the Madonna to save the man who was the enemy of her Divine Son, he implied in the plainest terms, that if Donato had been rescued by any power not human, it must have been by devils, who only saved their future victim from present death in order that he might add fresh crimes to those which he had already committed, and so be doomed to suffer more horribly for ever.

Powerful, however, as was the Capuchin's rhetoric, D'Urbino soon perceived that it was beginning to madden not a few of the men who heard him. Here and there the vast crowd began to sway to and fro, and an angry cry now and then broke forth in contradiction of the preacher's charges. At last, when the Capuchin threw aside all reserve and proceeded to identify Donato with the Liberal party of Roman reformers, the blunder which he was committing was so evident, that many of the more prudent among the clericals present began to look annoyed, and ominously to shake their heads. D'Urbino himself, having special reasons of his own for keeping out of any political difficulties at the present moment, lost no time in pushing his way to the outskirts of the crowd, intending to linger awhile to watch what might be the result of the gathering agitation.

To his surprise and by no means to his gratification, he encountered Margaret and Helen, with Francesca in their train, under the protection of the servant Fernando, standing together near one of the entrances to the vast amphitheatre, and vainly attempting to hear the speaker's words.

Knowing that it was no moment for ceremony, he at once spoke to Margaret and Helen, and advised their departure, on the ground of the riot that was every instant threatening more and more evidently to break forth. They were still in doubt, when an explosion at the farther end of the amphitheatre startled the whole assemblage into momentary silence.

The sound was slight, and was meant to frighten rather than injure, but it might be followed by another far more serious.

"For heaven's sake," cried D'Urbino, the moment he heard the ominous sound, "make haste home;" and taking command of the party without hesitation, he bade Fernando precede the cousins, and clear a free passage for them. He himself would follow instantly, he added, and would take charge of Francesca. Relying both upon his will and his power to fulfil the promise, Margaret and Helen at once walked on, following in the steps of Fernando, who showed no small dexterity as a pioneer under difficulties. They had not proceeded, however, more than forty or fifty yards, when, pausing to see whether D'Urbino and Francesca were behind them, they found that neither the one nor the other was to be seen. At the same time a fresh explosion, followed by the loud roar of an angry multitude, convinced them that the dreaded fray was actually beginning. At length, after lingering a few minutes, in the hope of seeing Francesca safe under the guardianship of D'Urbino, while the tumult was deepening and spreading, they felt that there was nothing for it but to hasten homewards without further delay.

D'Urbino and his charge had undoubtedly disappeared.

CHAPTER VII.

THE ARRIVAL AND ITS RESULTS.

The short winter's day was rapidly waning, as the two cousins found themselves within sight of home. To their surprise they saw a carriage drawn up before the door, from which a gentleman sprang vigorously to the ground, and began looking about him, apparently to make sure that he had arrived at his intended destination.

"If it were not for that energetic jump," said Margaret to her cousin, "I should be certain that this is none other than Mr. Charles Evelyn. What can have brought him to Rome just at this very time?"

"Who can account for the movements of

a professional idler like Mr. Evelyn?" rejoined Helen. "Probably he found his own companionship too much for him, and he has come for the purpose of bestowing his tediousness upon us, out of pure charity to himself."

The subject of the brief discussion had in the meantime disappeared within the doorway, and the cousins hastily followed him.

"It is, indeed, the unexpected gentleman himself!" exclaimed Helen, as they entered the drawing-room, and found Evelyn just seating himself, and beginning a history of his past movements for the benefit of her aunt. His only reply was to jump from his chair and shake hands heartily with Helen and Margaret, and then to fling himself upon a sofa, as if exhausted with fatigue. The salutations over, Helen began to recount the adventures of the afternoon with no little eagerness.

"What!" cried Evelyn, very unceremoniously interrupting her; "you have positively walked from one end of Rome to the other, for the sole purpose of hearing a man preach in the Coliseum! The very thought of it is a weariness to the flesh. But you were always frightfully active, Miss Sandford; and Miss Osborne was always nearly as bad. Life is really too short for such exploits."

"Yet do you know that when we first caught sight of you, leaping from your carriage," said Helen, " we almost decided that so energetic a gentleman could not possibly be the *dolce far niente* Mr. Evelyn with whom we have the happiness to be acquainted."

"Certainly it was a needless waste of energy, I must admit," replied he; "but then, you know that no man is ever perfectly consistent. If Homer is permitted sometimes to sleep, why should not Charles Evelyn be allowed sometimes to be in a hurry?"

Helen laughed, and Margaret assured him

that for herself she was beginning to find Rome the most exciting place in the whole world.

"What an illusion!" ejaculated Evelyn. "Do you know that the Romans themselves, who are fond of all sorts of little verbal quips and witticisms, make an anagram out of the word *Roma*, turning it into *Mora*, which is the Latin for 'delay.'"

"I think we know enough Latin to be aware of that fact," rejoined Helen, with a laugh.

"What!" exclaimed Evelyn, "do you understand Latin? what astonishing puzzles women really are! And you have actually learnt Latin of your own accord, when you were not forced to it by the laws of some terrible school? What an extraordinary waste of brain-power!"

"How is it then that you have managed to survive the sufferings of your school-days, and to enjoy the florid health which you still seem to possess?" asked Helen.

"Solely by attending to two golden rules —never to do anything that you are not compelled to do, and never to do anything to-day which can be put off till to-morrow. Why do you laugh, Miss Osborne?" he continued; "Don't you believe me?"

"Not altogether," said Margaret.

"You think I don't act up to my principles; is that what you mean?" he asked.

"Not exactly," she replied.

"But pray tell me what you do mean," he answered.

Margaret shook her head, but said nothing

"Then you refuse to explain yourself?" he went on.

"I don't think you exactly understand yourself," she said, his manner evidently growing a little serious.

"You think so?" asked Evelyn.

"On the whole, yes! if you insist on an answer," said Margaret.

"Well, I promise you that I will act more

faithfully up to my principles as long as I stay in Rome. There is no place on earth like it, for an idle man like myself, with a tolerable income, and holding enlightened views of his duty towards himself."

"I should never be a convert to those views, at least in this wonderful city," observed Margaret.

"Is she as infatuated as ever, Miss Sandford, on things in general and on enjoyment in particular?" said Evelyn, turning to Helen.

"I fear there is not much amendment," replied Helen, with a pleasant smile.

"While there is life, however, there is hope," rejoined Evelyn, with a mock solemnity. "But the worst of it is that with your energetic and enthusiastic people, you cut short your life before you have really learnt how to make the best of it. And to think of the dreadful maxims instilled into us from our earliest childhood! Early to bed and early to rise, makes a man healthy, wealthy and wise. What a pernicious sentiment! Who can wonder at the miseries of life, when the ingenuous mind is thus corrupted from the beginning? To my mind, it is the great charm of Rome, that nobody is in time for anything."

"Nevertheless," interposed Mrs. Sandford, "I must remind you that unless you go at once and secure yourself lodgings, you will not be back in time for our dinner."

"You remind me of the last act of inconsistency of which I have been guilty, Mrs. Sandford," he rejoined. "Will you believe it, that, contrary to all my principles, I took rooms at a new hotel hard by, before I presented myself to you? My chief excuse is that it was the first hotel that I happened to see, and that being a new one, I was totally unacquainted with its character. Was not that an act of virtue almost heroic, Miss Osborne?" he added.

"Undoubtedly!" said Margaret, laughing.

"You should write a book, Mr. Evelyn, expounding your views on morality."

He was on the point of beginning to expound some fresh paradox, when he was cut short by the entrance of Fernando, to ask the young ladies whether they could tell Francesca's father why she had not returned home in their company. The mosaic-worker was below, said Fernando, and evidently anxious about his daughter. Would the Signora be good enough to come down and speak to him? A little alarmed, Margaret ran down stairs and told Giorgione all she knew, but he was only partially reassured by what she had to tell him, and expressed his intention of starting immediately to search for Francesca himself. Extracting from him a promise to let her know the moment he returned, Margaret went upstairs, by no means without anxiety as to what might have occurred. Her anxiety spread a cloud over the rest of the party, and the dinner that soon followed did little to dispel the gloom.

And the gloom would have been deeper still, if they had known what had been the final results of the preaching Capuchin's imprudent zeal. Remembering how short was the distance they had proceeded when they lost all sight of D'Urbino and Francesca, neither Margaret nor Helen could shake off the dread that they had been involved in some violent struggle between the partisans of the government and the liberal portion of the crowd. Nothing short of absolute compulsion, they felt confident, would have kept Francesca away from her father's house at a moment when his anxiety for her safety must be so intense. And as no tidings of her arrival reached them, and no inquiries after their own safety were made on the part of D'Urbino, their alarm grew more and more intolerable as the evening passed away.

Nor had they left the scene of the tumult a moment too soon. The second explosion which they had heard had been in itself as harmless as the first, being intended only to create alarm. But alarm in a Roman mob is apt to be intensified into terror, and at the same time to stir up the few fiercer spirits it may contain to savage fury. Whether, indeed, the explosions had been the work of the police or of the malcontents, it was never publicly ascertained.

The result unquestionably expected had instantly followed. The panic-stricken people, forgetting, or not knowing, that the vast area of the Coliseum was not really filled, and therefore still afforded protection from the storm that raged in the centre immediately around the fiery preacher and his military protectors, crowded madly through the narrow entrances, trampling on those who fell in the rush, till from sheer exhaustion they paused in their struggles. Some scores of men and women were more or less seriously injured, and some few were taken up dead when the amphitheatre and its entrances were finally cleared. How many were wounded and how many killed was of course kept a secret by the authorities, for the truth-telling of English newspaper reporters is a thing as odious in the eyes of the Roman government as the freedom of English thought.

All around the platform on which the preacher had stood, a hand to hand fight raged between the liberals and their enemies for several minutes. Of the police and the soldiers a few were cut down, or stabbed, or otherwise wounded. But the victory was with the "guardians of order," as they were styled in the government journals, which told the story after their own version. Two of the malcontents were left dead, and at least a score were seized and consigned to the prison cells, from whence they were to be brought to receive the sentences preordained by "justice" on behalf of the dull and ignorant despotism against which they were presumed to have been deliberately conspiring.

In the meantime the reports which flew from mouth to mouth were as exaggerated as such rumours inevitably become, where suspicion and ill-will are the chronic disorders of the time. Rome was in flames, said one story; his Holiness had fled, said another; two hundred political malcontents had been arrested, said a third. By-and-bye, reports reached the extreme parts of the city, and the Sandford party were beginning to feel almost as much agitated as the Romans themselves, when they were startled by the sight of the terror-stricken Giorgione rushing unannounced into the room where they sat, to ask if they had yet heard tidings of his child.

He had been to the scene of the tumult and had found it totally deserted. He had next been to the prison where the captured rioters were lodged, and being (secretly) on friendly terms with more than one of the police officials, had ascertained that nothing whatever had been heard of D'Urbino or of

Francesca herself. In fact, unless they had returned into the midst of the crowd the moment they had parted with Helen and Margaret, it was impossible that they could have been involved in the rush of the multitude, or in the fight around the platform. Various women who had seen the dead and wounded carried away, one and all agreed that no persons corresponding to the descriptions of D'Urbino and Francesca were among either the injured or the killed.

As the miserable father told his story, the calm attention of one of the listeners rapidly changed to serious alarm. Happening to turn for a moment towards Evelyn, Margaret was astonished to note the look of mingled dread and anger which his countenance assumed, and the keen closing of the lips and stern knitting of the brow with which he proceeded to disentangle the details of Giorgione's somewhat incoherent account. Then, as soon as he had satisfied himself, he quietly asked Margaret to give him five minutes conversation in another room. Not a little surprised, she immediately granted the request.

"Can you tell me anything," he began, as soon as they were alone, "about the relations between this man's daughter and the gentleman in whose charge you were compelled to leave her?"

"I know very little about it," replied Margaret, "except that for some time she has been sitting to him as a model for an ideal bust upon which he is engaged. He is a sculptor, as you have heard us mention this evening."

"What knowledge have you of his personal character?" continued Evelyn.

"Not very much indeed," said Margaret. "We met him first at the French Embassy, and from what I saw of him I certainly became interested in him, and he has been here occasionally since."

"I don't mean that exactly," said Evelyn. "Do you believe him to be an honourable man, and a fit person to have the charge of a girl at such a juncture?"

"So far as I can judge, certainly," replied Margaret.

"Is the girl good-looking?" he asked.

"Singularly so—at least in my judgment," said Margaret.

"It is not likely that she is at this moment with him in his studio?" Evelyn continued. "Where does he live?"

"In the Via Felice, not five minutes' walk from here," she replied.

"Tell me the number of the house," said Evelyn.

"For that you must ask the girl's father himself," replied Margaret, and they returned to the rest of the party. Looking more grave than ever, Evelyn at once took the hand of the mosaic-worker with a respectful tenderness, and led him out of the room.

"Of course you have been to Signor D'Urbino's house to inquire if your daughter is there?" he said, as they went down the stairs.

"Nothing had been heard of the Cavaliere or of my unhappy child," replied Giorgione.

"You have confidence in D'Urbino's honour?" again asked Evelyn.

"The most undoubted confidence," said Giorgione.

"It is more than I have," said Evelyn to himself, with rising feelings of disgust and anger against one, of whom he knew nothing, but whom he began to suspect of the basest treachery. At the mere suspicion of such treachery all the latent manliness of Evelyn's nature was stirred to its depths; and ascertaining from Giorgione where D'Urbino lived, he instantly started on his search, to the utter amazement of Margaret and Helen.

In a few minutes Evelyn was in full conversation with D'Urbino's housekeeper, whom he frightened out of all composure by the vehemence of the questioning with which he followed up her statement that neither her master nor Francesca had been seen since the early part of the afternoon.

"Does the girl often come here?" he asked.

"Oftener than I say she ought to come," replied Betta. "And it is often too that I tell him she shall never come inside his doors again, as long as I am here. There! Eccellenza," she went on, throwing open the door of D'Urbino's studio. "Look there! there she is, in all her impudence!" and the jealous old woman pointed to the bust of the missing girl, as it had been left uncovered after the morning's sitting.

The beauty and refinement of the face struck the quick perception of the accomplished Evelyn, and he was still in silent contemplation of its charm, when a loud knocking startled him from his thoughts, and three men strode into the studio, and were at once recognised by Betta, as emissaries of the police.

"You are not the Cavaliere D'Urbino, I believe," said their leader to Evelyn, without an attempt at ceremony."

"I am not," rejoined Evelyn; "but I am here for the very purpose of finding him. For Heaven's sake say where he is? and where is Francesca Giorgione?"

"I know nothing of either of them," replied the man. "We are here on a duty, which must be instantly attended to. There is the order authorising our search for suspected papers; and if you have any sense, you will tell this foolish old woman, who stands staring there, to leave off wringing her hands, and help us to do our duty. Come, my friend," he continued, speaking to Betta, "you will do your master most good by saving us the disagreeable work of breaking open locks and doors, and if you do happen to know where he keeps his letters, you could save a world of time, by taking us to the place without a word more."

Trembling with fear, and yet with a hope

that by betraying her master's secrets she would be working for his soul's health, Betta without more ado pointed out the cabinet in which, as she was well aware, from her habits of stealthy watching, D'Urbino certainly did deposit sundry letters and documents. It was, in fact, the only piece of furniture in any one of his rooms which he kept always locked, and to which she had not free access. The police agent immediately turned the handle of the door, and to Betta's astonishment found it unlocked, and its shelves completely empty

"*Santa Vergine!*" she cried out: "I saw him lock it safely this very morning."

"Come, come, my clever friend," rejoined the man, "the trick is too plain. Be good enough to show us the inside of every box, closet and shelf belonging to the Cavaliere, or else—" and he whispered something in the ear of the unlucky Betta, which speedily quickened her movements. The search was complete, but unavailing. No one suspected the real hiding place of the incriminating papers, and the baffled agents departed in no amiable mood at their discomfiture. As they left the house, Evelyn remembered the proverbial weakness of Italian officials, and soon overtaking them, lightly tapped the shoulder of the chief man of the three. A very brief and muttered conversation ensued, ending in the transfer of a small gold coin from the pocket of Evelyn to the hand of the police agent, accompanied with a nod of intelligence to his two companions.

"At any rate no harm will be done," said Evelyn to himself, "even if the story is altogether falsehood, and they know no more of D'Urbino than I do."

Thus meditating, he followed silently in the steps of the three agents, his thoughts recurring again and again to the portrait he had been contemplating.

CHAPTER VIII.

ARRESTED.

Yet never were suspicions more groundless than those entertained by Evelyn in respect to D'Urbino's conduct towards Francesca. When she left the Coliseum by his side, following the rest of the party as rapidly as the crowd would allow them, D'Urbino had noticed that she looked deadly pale, and she returned no answer to the reassuring words with which he attempted to convince her that no danger was really to be apprehended. He attributed both the pallor and the silence to the same cause which had produced her late agitation in his own studio, and said nothing more.

They had not, however, proceeded more than some fifty or sixty yards, when he began to suspect that their progress was being intentionally hindered by certain persons in the throng, but whose countenances were unknown to him. First one rough-looking personage would attempt to cross the road immediately in their front, and though the attempt failed, it answered the purpose of delaying their advance. Then another man, also a stranger, addressed D'Urbino, with some trivial inquiries as to what had been passing in the Coliseum, to create the unusual disturbance in the streets.

D'Urbino's angry remonstrances at being thus hindered in his efforts to keep up with the two cousins, were unnoticed, apparently, by his questioner, and yet he felt convinced that this man had some hidden motive in addressing him. Francesca, too, began to grow more alarmed; and was so convinced that they were being dogged, that in her fright she broke through every law of

Roman etiquette, and clung to D'Urbino's arm for support. Annoyed as he was at the girl's extreme fear, incomprehensible, as he thought it, in a character of so much power and self-control, he had not the heart to bid her loosen her hold.

At the first cross street which they reached, he turned rapidly out of the main thoroughfare, intending to strike across to the gardens of the Quirinal, and so reach the *Via dellequattro fontane* by comparatively unfrequented streets. Margaret and Helen were by this time so completely out of sight that all attempt to overtake them was hopeless, and he had only to consider how to conduct Francesca unmolested to her father's house, and then betake himself to his studio, and learn what had been the fate of his compromising papers.

Fast as they walked, however, others walked faster still. Within a couple of minutes they found themselves overtaken by half-a-dozen men, wearing the government uniform, who at once bade D'Urbino consider himself their prisoner. It was bootless to think of flight, even if he could have deserted Francesca at such a moment; and resistance would have been an act of madness. He therefore turned to the terrified Francesca, and uttering the ominous word "arrested," inquired of the leader of his captors where he was to be taken, and what was the charge against him.

"The Signore will be good enough to attend us in peace," replied the official, "and he will soon obtain answers to both his questions; and in the meantime I would advise both haste and silence."

After vainly urging Francesca to leave him and hasten home with all speed, D'Urbino obeyed the injunction, and was conducted to what seemed a private house in a quiet street near the Quirinal Palace. There the party stopped, Francesca still lingering in their rear. The door of the house was instantly opened, their approach having evidently been watched for from within, and again entreating Francesca to seek her home without delay, D'Urbino was desired to enter the house, his captors following him, and the door was closed behind them.

Without a word, he was led into a room at the back of the building, its one window opening upon a small court-yard, surrounded with walls, so that even if he could have forced his way through the iron bars which forbade all egress through the window itself, escape would still have been impossible. The room was plainly meant for business, and not for enjoyment, a table and a few chairs constituting its whole furniture. Here D'Urbino was left alone, his conductors refusing to reply to his questions, even with a single word, and locking the room door behind them as they left him to his very unpleasant meditations.

He was still racking his brain to find some explanation of this sudden seizure, and wondering who could have been playing the traitor against him, when he heard the key of the door quietly and slowly turned in the lock, as if the person turning it wished to enter without noise. Wondering what could be the object of the attempted silence, D'Urbino held his breath, and, though unarmed, stood upon his guard against the suspected violence. The door quietly opened, and a tall and well-dressed personage entered so rapidly that D'Urbino could not catch his features as he turned to close the door as noiselessly as possible. Then the new comer moved hastily towards D'Urbino, who at once recognised the well known and dreaded *Cameriere di Spada*, Giovanni Rinaldo himself.

"Did you receive a note this morning?" asked Rinaldo, speaking in English.

The amazement with which D'Urbino received the question did not prevent him from immediately replying, also in English:

"I did receive it."

"Have you acted on it?" continued Rinaldo.

"I have," he replied.

"Both as to your person and your rooms?" asked Rinaldo.

"As to both of them," answered D'Urbino.

"Then fear nothing, and answer nothing."

And so saying, he opened the door as quietly as before, went out, and cautiously locked it. Almost instantly afterwards, D'Urbino heard the door of the house opened, apparently with ostentatious noise, and then shut with an equal absence of all attempt at concealment. More bewildered than ever, D'Urbino continued pacing up and down the room, and wondering how long he was to be kept in his intolerable state of suspense. He thought over the whole history of his connexion with the liberal and revolutionary party in Rome, and tried to recollect any overt act into which he might have been betrayed, and any indiscreet words that he might have uttered, which would have furnished some decent pretext for his arrest and future punishment; but he could recall nothing of the kind.

His intimacy with the men who controlled the action of the anti-clerical party was of recent date, and he had never been admitted into their innermost secrets. He was acquainted personally with but few of their number, his communications with them being for the most part carried on through the mosaic-worker, Giorgione; and though he knew it not, it was partly through the insight into his character which Giorgione thus obtained, that the latter had been induced to permit Francesca's frequent visits to the young sculptor's studio for professional purposes.

D'Urbino's revolutionary views were, moreover, very far removed from those of the more violent of the party, with whom he nevertheless felt it his duty to act, and whom he was prepared to obey. Of this difference between himself and the secret committees, or clubs, which controlled the situation, he was, indeed, painfully aware; and as he strode up and down the dismal room, in which he was now confined, he could not resist a suspicion that possibly his arrest was due to some treachery on their part, and that he was being offered up as a victim, in order to draw the attention of the Government from others far more dangerous than himself, and restrained by none of his scruples or his fastidious sense of honour.

But what was the possible explanation of the proceedings of the Cameriere Rinaldo? Was he the basest of all the base tools of a tyrannical and unscrupulous government? or was he honestly anxious to save D'Urbino from the consequences of his own heedlessness? And on the last supposition, what could be the motive of his interference? Who was this Rinaldo, to whom so much evil was imputed, and of whom so little was known? What was his personal history, before he originally appeared in Rome, in the character of a reformer and anti-clerical partisan? D'Urbino himself was of a younger generation, and could not recollect the days when Rinaldo first joined the revolutionary movement. It was all a mystery; and having absolutely no materials from which to construct a consistent hypothesis as to the motives which guided Rinaldo's incomprehensible proceedings, D'Urbino finally decided that he would take his sincerity for granted, and act upon his advice, inexplicable as his proceedings were in themselves.

D'Urbino had only just made up his mind as to the course he would pursue, when the door again opened, and a gentlemanly looking person entered, followed by two men, evidently of the ordinary level of inferior police officials. His manner towards D'Urbino took the young sculptor by surprise. With a polite bow he begged D'Urbino to be seated, while he himself sat down at the table. D'Urbino, who was prepared for a display of the traditional violence and insults which the minions of blood-thirsty tyrants are in the habit of offering to the victims of their oppression, hardly knew how to conduct himself. Instead of delivering himself of the indignant invectives which he had been contemplating, he took a seat, as requested, feeling something like a foolish school boy in the presence of his master.

"I have the pleasure of speaking to the Cavaliere D'Urbino," said the questioner, in a tone of enquiry,

D'Urbino signified his assent.

"Living, and working as a sculptor, in the Via Felice?" continued the other.

"The same," responded D'Urbino.

"Unmarried?" asked the official.

"Yes," replied D'Urbino.

"Until lately, the Cavaliere's sister, the Signora Bianca, has lived with him," continued the other.

"Until lately," replied D'Urbino.

"At present the Signora does not live with you?"

"At present she does not live with me," he replied.

"I have an unpleasant duty to perform," continued the very polite personage, whose inclination of the head, as D'Urbino replied to his queries, was a perfect model of courtesy. "I must request Signor D'Urbino to permit himself to be searched. He must be aware that this personal searching is a necessity in all political investigations."

"I submit, of course—resistance would be useless," rejoined D'Urbino, and the two attendants proceeded at once to rifle every pocket in his garments. The proceeding was unpleasant enough, though carried out without rudeness, and it was only the secret sense of triumph with which D'Urbino watched the disappointed faces of the searchers, that prevented his writhing under what he felt to be a gross personal indignity.

"Signor D'Urbino is a man of honour," said the person in authority, when nothing was produced of a suspicious nature; "will he pledge me his word that he has no papers secreted about him which have escaped the examination to which he has been submitted? We have known cases in which nothing less than the cutting open of a gentleman's dress has revealed the papers for which search has been made."

"On my honour I have nothing of the kind," rejoined D'Urbino, without a moment's hesitation, and with a look of being secretly amused at the fruitless nature of the investigation.

"What, then, is the cause of your amusement, Cavaliere?" asked the other, a little puzzled what to do.

"Simply because I never carry about with me any compromising papers," replied D'Urbino.

"Not even—" began his questioner, and then suddenly paused. Then after a little thought, he directed the searchers to leave the room and wait outside till they were summoned. Then, in a lower tone, he took up his broken sentence. " Not even when expecting to meet your friends, Cavaliere, at a foreign ambassador's ball?" he said, with a significant smile.

The recollection of the little volume of English verses, with its pencilled list of initials, and of the conversation with Rinaldo, with its sudden and only partially accounted for close, flashed across D'Urbino's thoughts, and for the first time in the interview his heart beat fast and painfully. Looking steadily into the face of his questioner, his eyelids almost drooped before the penetrating gaze which was fastened upon him. But the heart-beating and the feeling of shrinking rapidly gave way before his resolute will, as he replied—

" I have to correct my statement in regard to one occasion. It is useless, I suppose," he continued, " to ask who and what you are, or how you come to be acquainted with my private life; or I could ask whether you were yourself at the ball you speak of."

"In one sense I was there; in another I was not there," he answered.

"You imply that you have acquired some information as to my conduct on that occasion."

"I do," said his questioner.

"Was the information communicated to you by some person present there?"

"It was communicated to me by two persons present there. More than this I am unable to inform you."

"Men, or women?" D'Urbino asked.

"So far I do not mind answering you," said the other. "They were women."

He then called to the attendants outside to come in.

"Are they yet returned?" he asked.

"Not yet, Signore," replied one of the men.

"Let me know the moment they appear."

Again alone with D'Urbino, he continued the conversation in the same quiet manner as before, but it struck D'Urbino that his examination was really ended, and that his companion was talking against time, and that he himself was in some way connected with the return of the expected party. At length he ventured on a direct question.

"May I ask," he said, "if I am to be released on the return of the persons you were just now speaking of?"

"I fear I can make no promise, but it is just possible."

"I think I am aware of the business on which they are being employed," suggested D'Urbino.

"Indeed?" said his companion. "May I ask what is your guess?"

"They are gone to my house to make the same search among my possessions which you have just completed about my person."

"You think so?" asked the other. "What are your reasons for the supposition?"

"I was aware that it was highly probable that such a search would be made."

A slight shade of surprise crossed the face of his questioner, who at once added—

"Possibly you were warned beforehand."

"Possibly."

"May I ask if you are perfectly easy as to the discoveries that would be made on the hypothesis that your surmise is correct?"

"Perfectly so."

"When was the warning given to you?" asked the other, hoping to take D'Urbino by surprise by the sudden question.

"What warning?" asked D'Urbino, with a complete affectation of astonishment. "I never told you that I received any warning. I merely admitted the possibility of such a thing."

"You are a clever fellow, Cavaliere," replied his companion, "and would do honour to our profession. And you know that our numbers are not over-stocked at present. I presume that the calling of a sculptor is not extraordinarily profitable."

"Nevertheless it is an honourable calling," rejoined D'Urbino, with a marked emphasis on the word honourable.

"Is it a dishonourable thing to act in the service of the law, order, and religion?" continued the other. And so saying, he rose and left the room, turning the key as he shut the door behind him. Whether it was half an hour or an hour, or even more, before he returned, D'Urbino could not tell. It was so unwonted a sensation to be shut up in a dimly-lighted cell-like room, with the conviction that his home was being searched for evidence of his complicity in what might be counted a treasonable conspiracy, that it was not easy to calculate the lapse of time with any trustworthy accuracy. At last, however, his suspense came to an end. His late inquisitor returned and informed him politely that no discoveries had been made; adding, at the same time, that an English gentleman was anxious to see him on important business.

"But surely," cried D'Urbino with unconcealed irritation, "I am now to be set free."

"It is impossible, Cavaliere," said the other; "I have my report to draw up, and without further instructions I must detain you here."

"In this miserable cell, do you mean?" exclaimed D'Urbino. "Can you wonder that the government you serve is abhorred by every Roman who has a spark of manhood in him?"

"There are two opinions on the subject," replied the other, unmoved. "But Cavaliere D'Urbino need be under no apprehensions of ungentlemanly usage. He will find tolerably pleasant accommodation upstairs, in which more than one prince has slept under similar circumstances. The Cavaliere will be informed when his supper is served. I have the honour to wish you good night."

And with a polite obeisance he left the room.

D'Urbino's visitor was immediately introduced. The two men at once saw that they were strangers to each other. After a somewhat stiff mutual salutation, the visitor began:—

"My name is Evelyn. I am speaking, I believe, to Cavaliere D'Urbino."

"Such is my name," replied D'Urbino, by no means conciliated by the undisguised hauteur with which he was addressed. "What is your business with me?"

"To inquire after a young woman, of the name of Francesca Giorgione."

"May I ask by whose desire you have undertaken the inquiry?" said D'Urbino. "You are personally unknown to me, Mr. Evelyn."

"But I am not personally unknown to a family with whom you have some slight acquaintance—Mrs. Sandford, her daughter, and her niece."

"Your information does not assist me to a conclusion. I have no means of testing the truth of your statement."

"Then you decline to give me any intelligence of the young woman in question," said Evelyn, with rising irritation at thus unexpectedly finding his word doubted.

"I refuse nothing at all, Mr. Evelyn," rejoined D'Urbino, as haughtily as the other. "If you are really a friend of Mrs. and Miss Sandford and Miss Osborne, you must be aware that certain credentials are necessary in making such a demand upon one who never saw you in his life before."

Taken completely aback by so unlooked-for a reception, Evelyn stared for a few moments at D'Urbino, and then seating himself on a chair, replied, "You are right, Signore; the fault is my own. What can I do or say to convince you that I am not,—well, how shall I put it?—an impostor?"

"That rests with yourself," replied D'Urbino, with forbidding coldness.

"Shall I tell you why I came here, and how I learnt where you were to be found?"

"As you may think best yourself," said D'Urbino, indifferently.

Utterly provoked, Evelyn again gave way to his anger, and went on committing blunder after blunder.

"Do you know what you are charged with, Signor D'Urbino?" he cried fiercely.

"I believe I am here on a charge of disloyalty to the present Roman government," replied D'Urbino.

"Is that all you believe?" asked Evelyn, with an eloquent sneer.

"I can suspect no other accusation," rejoined D'Urbino, still so calm, that Evelyn was already hating him as the very incarnation of hypocrisy.

"Do you not know that you are suspected of having carried off this deluded girl from the custody of her miserable father?"

"Who is it that suspects me?" asked D'Urbino, with a cynical smile.

"I do," rejoined Evelyn, a little disconcerted at the question.

"Indeed!" replied D'Urbino. "Who else suspects me?" he continued. "Does the girl's father suspect me?"

Evelyn recalled Giorgione's words, and replied—

"No, he does not."

"Does Mrs. Sandford?"

"No, I believe not."

"Does Miss Sandford?"

"No, not that I know of."

"Does Miss Osborne?"

"I have not heard that she does."

"This, then, is the exact state of the case, as it really stands," rejoined D'Urbino; "an English stranger, whose name I never heard before, visits me in a police cell, and tells me to my face that he thinks me guilty of an atrocious crime, of which the father and the English friends of the girl in question do not for a moment suspect me. Suppose, Mr. Evelyn, that the tables are turned, and that I ask you what is *your* motive in coming to me with this monstrous and grossly insolent accusation."

What with the force of this reply, and the quiet energy with which D'Urbino spoke, all the while fixing his eyes with unswerving gaze upon Evelyn's countenance, Evelyn was abashed and confounded. He said nothing, and looked so utterly discomfited, that D'Urbino, feeling and enjoying his triumph, went on in another strain.

"Come, Mr. Evelyn," he said, almost smiling, "you have made a mistake. I see you are an honest man, I will tell you all I know of poor Francesca. She is a noble-hearted girl, and I most sincerely hope that no harm has happened to her."

"The Signore's supper is served," said a servant, entering unceremoniously, but without any rudeness of manner. "If the Signore will be good enough to proceed at once to the rooms he is to occupy for the night, he will find everything ready."

"Does this mean that I am to go about my business?" asked Evelyn, abruptly.

"I am desired to inform Signor Evelyn that if he has not finished his conversation, he may remain with Cavaliere D'Urbino until his supper is ended," replied the man.

"Shall I be intruding?" asked Evelyn of D'Urbino, every trace of his hauteur having vanished.

D'Urbino at once acceded, and they mounted to the rooms that were to be his prison for the night.

CHAPTER IX.

WITHIN AND WITHOUT THE POLICE COURT.

"And this is the fare provided by a paternal despotism, for its subjects clapped in prison merely on suspicion," exclaimed D'Urbino, as he sat down to the meal provided for him. "It might be worse apparently. Let us drink to our better acquaintance, Mr. Evelyn," he added, pouring out a glass of wine and offering it to his visitor. "The wine is no doubt poor enough, but it will serve as a pledge in the absence of anything better."

Evelyn took the glass, and the two men exchanged expressions of good will.

"Will you help me to test the qualities of Roman prison cookery?" continued D'Urbino; "or, will you sit and ask me any questions you wish to have answered?"

Evelyn declined the offer, still almost suspecting that D'Urbino was attempting to put him off with vague talk, in order to conceal his knowledge of Francesca's fate. However, D'Urbino's candid manner soon disabused him, and he listened with mingled pain and pleasure to D'Urbino's account of his arrest and of his parting with Francesca at the door of the house, in which he was a prisoner.

"I assure you," D'Urbino continued, "that I was utterly amazed when I heard from you that she had not long ago arrived at her father's house. She insisted, against my remonstrances, on following us here, and then again I urged her instant return home. I cannot imagine any reason whatever for her delay."

"Is she in the habit of going about

Rome very much by herself?" asked Evelyn.

"I should suppose so," replied D'Urbino. "It is the way with other young women of her class in life."

"Have you any clue as to her special reasons for following you as far as this?"

"To tell you the truth, I never thought much about it at all. Now you ask me, I suppose it must have been in the expectation that I should come out again immediately; or if I was detained, with a good-natured intention of telling my friends how I had been disposed of. She is a singularly warmhearted girl, and with far more forethought than Roman women in general."

Notwithstanding the perfect frankness with which D'Urbino spoke, Evelyn still harboured his suspicion that some tie existed between the young sculptor and his captivating model, which was unknown to any but themselves. As the conversation did not proceed without sundry breaks, owing to D'Urbino's devotion to his supper, Evelyn resolved to venture upon a little cautious examination, framing his questions with the deliberation which the process of D'Urbino's eating and drinking allowed.

"The girl is certainly singularly handsome," he observed.

D'Urbino looked up at him with a look of surprise, that convinced Evelyn that some sort of secret was in existence.

"How on earth do you know that?" asked D'Urbino. "Have you ever seen her? I thought you implied just now that you had not been in Rome for some years, and only returned this afternoon."

"If I say that I was in your studio this evening, you can understand that I am not ignorant of Francesca's beauty."

"Mr. Evelyn," rejoined D'Urbino, not a little nettled, "may I ask by what right you intruded into my house in my absence? Surely you must be aware that it was a most unwarrantable proceeding."

"I was directed there by the girl's father, who authorised me to call and inquire if you had yet returned," said Evelyn.

"I do not see how that accounts for your intrusion into my private rooms," rejoined D'Urbino, as angry as ever.

"Your housekeeper took me into your studio," said Evelyn, "and pointed out to me a nearly finished bust, with the information that it was the girl whom I was in quest of."

"I am willing to overlook a good deal that is strange in your conduct, Mr. Evelyn," rejoined D'Urbino, "but am I to understand that you questioned my servant as to the movements of Francesca Giorgione?"

"I confess that I did so," replied Evelyn, feeling by no means particularly easy under D'Urbino's angry eyes.

"As you had no scruple in discussing my private affairs with a woman in my service," said D'Urbino, "you can have no scruple in informing me what were her replies to your catechising."

"Certainly not," replied Evelyn; "her one idea seemed to be that Francesca's visits to your studio were more improper, and in fact scandalous."

"I am aware that she thinks so," observed D'Urbino, curtly. "Did she supply you with any further information, or treat you with the reserve due towards one who was practically a spy upon my affairs? I say practically, Mr. Evelyn," he continued, noticing the flush of anger with which Evelyn heard the angry and insulting word.

"I understand you," rejoined Evelyn, "and accept the explanation. What more she might have said, I cannot tell. I was still examining the bust, and let me add, with no small admiration, when a party of the police appeared, on an errand which you clearly had anticipated."

"And did you remain during the search they instituted?" asked D'Urbino, eagerly.

"I did; and when it was over, it was by the judicious administration of an English sovereign that I learnt your present confinement."

"I have been told already that nothing was found to inculpate me in any way," replied D'Urbino; "but lying in this unhappy city is so nearly universal, that the report may be totally false, and meant to throw me off my guard. But I am puzzled to understand how you came to think that I was expecting the search. How can you assume that I had anything to hide?"

"Your servant pointed out the cabinet where she said you usually kept letters and papers. She told the police that it was certainly locked in the morning, and when they were preparing to force the lock, it opened in their hands, and there was nothing to be seen."

"Two more questions, and I will ask no more," returned D'Urbino. "You speak as if my servant was disposed to betray me to the police agents: you will do me a service if you will give me your impression without reserve."

"My impression was that you should be cautious in your dealings with that woman."

"If that woman is playing me false," said D'Urbino, "she is an atrocious and ungrateful hypocrite. But of that we need say no more. You were present, I gather from what you said, during the whole of the examination of my rooms?"

"Throughout the whole," said Evelyn.

"Was any injury done to my busts, or casts, or to the model of Francesca?"

"None whatever," replied Evelyn. "Your furniture was examined with the most ruthless curiosity, every closet was searched, and the very floors were keenly looked at; but no mischief was done to the works you must most value as an enthusiastic artist. And now, Signor D'Urbino, you must allow me to ask you in return one or two questions of my own, which I had not the remotest idea of putting to you when I left my friends the Sandfords, but which are forced upon me by what you now have said. If you think that I am taking an unwarrantable liberty in asking these questions, you have only to say so, and I am silent for the future. But if you are the man of honour and of good feeling which I take you to be, you will at least forgive me for what I am about to ask you."

"I will gladly answer anything that is fitting that a stranger should ask me," answered D'Urbino, with unpromising coldness.

"Therein lies my difficulty," replied Evelyn; "you know nothing of me except what I tell you myself."

D'Urbino bowed, but said nothing.

"I am an old friend of Mrs. Sandford and of her daughter and her niece," continued Evelyn.

"So I understand from yourself," replied D'Urbino, with unmistakeable meaning.

"Well! at any rate, I can but repeat that I take a deep interest in all that concerns them; and I should add that as they are much interested in the girl Francesca—"

"Indeed?" interrupted D'Urbino, "I was not aware of the fact."

Evelyn, again puzzled by D'Urbino's changes of manner, looked at him with renewed suspicion.

"There is nothing to suspect, Mr. Evelyn," said D'Urbino, returning the gaze. "I merely expressed my surprise at the existence of feelings which I had never heard mentioned."

"Are you then so much in the confidence of Miss Osborne and her friends," asked Evelyn, "that you should know their thoughts about every chance Roman acquaintance of a rank in life unequal to their own?"

"I understand your sneer," rejoined D'Urbino, "I have only a slight acquaintance with the ladies, who, as you inform me, are your intimate friends. But as the girl Francesca has been sitting to me for an ideal bust at intervals for some months, and as she talks to me with perfect freedom about all her friends and acquaintances, I am surprised that I have seldom heard her mention the names of the Sandfords or of Miss Osborne, especially as she lives close by, on the supposition that they take so much interest in her welfare."

"There may have been a motive," suggested Evelyn.

"I know of none whatever," said D'Urbino. "You will oblige me by proceeding with your questions."

"Briefly then," proceeded Evelyn, "may I assure my friends that you are not implicated in any of the treasonable conspiracies against the existing government of Rome; and that Francesca is not an instrument in your hands for dangerous purposes?"

"A truly modest request!" exclaimed D'Urbino, "and from a gentleman, who, though he speaks Italian remarkably well, is evidently an Englishman, but has not even produced a card to identify himself, so far as such a ceremony is of any value."

"Then you decline to answer me," rejoined Evelyn, in manifest irritation.

"Pardon me," returned D'Urbino, with provoking composure. "You are as hasty as if you were a hot-blooded Italian. I never declined to answer you. I was about to say that inimitably cool as are your queries, I can answer them to your satisfaction. You are at liberty to inform my acquaintances, Mrs. and Miss Sandford and Miss Osborne, who you say are also your intimate friends, that I am not implicated in any treasonable conspiracy whatever, though I would support any rational scheme for a radical change of system. And as to employing an admirable girl like Francesca Giorgione as a tool for political ends, the charge is one, which if ever you come to know me better, you will be profoundly ashamed for having insinuated.

"And now, to show you I bear no ill-will towards you on account of your offensive questions, I will ask you to do me a kindness. I expect to be a free man again to-morrow morning, so far as it is possible to be a free man, or even a man at all, in this long-suffering city; and in that case I shall instantly satisfy myself about the safety of Francesca Giorgione. But if I am still kept a prisoner, you will gratify me by bringing me any information you can obtain. In the meantime, there is my hand."

With mingled feelings of pleasure, annoyance, and bewilderment, Evelyn shook the hand that was offered, and straightway went his way, with a disagreeable consciousness that this young Roman sculptor had made him feel 'smaller' than he had ever felt in his whole previous life, from his school-days until now.

In the mean time a meeting had taken place outside the secret police court in which D'Urbino was detained, which was destined to exercise an influence on his life, far more lasting than any that could be the direct result of his arrest and temporary imprisonment. When the Cameriere left him, and passed, as he had correctly surmised, into the open air, noisily shutting the house door behind him, few persons still remained in the neighbouring streets. After a brief glance around him, Rinaldo walked away. His eye, however, was attracted by the appearance of a young woman, who met him within a few steps of the house he had left. An expression of singular distress and weariness could not blind him to the fact that she was strikingly handsome, nor did the listless languor of her movements conceal the grace and natural elasticity of her figure.

As she came near, she seemed half inclined to pause and speak to him, but after an almost momentary though intelligent look into his face, she appeared to change her mind, and they passed each other without further notice. He was absent from two to three hours, and when he returned, the moon was up, and flooding the churches, palaces and fountains of the city with that soft radiance which is unknown in northern latitudes, and under which that wonderful union of the past and the present, of the dead and the living, which is the one great characteristic of the Eternal city, presents itself in all its most captivating beauty. Its effect upon Rinaldo, at all times a man open to such impressions, was profoundly sad. Beauty, he knew only too well, at all times saddened him; and especially that beauty which lingers about the relics of past ages, and which at once is eloquent on the unity of the thoughts and passions of the dead and of the living, and on the utter vanity of all merely temporary hopes and fears.

As he drew towards his destination, he lingered for a few minutes near a small fountain on which the moonbeams were falling, and making its millions of drops sparkle with a dazzling light. A few fragments of antique sculpture, too much injured to be worth a place in a gallery or a museum, had been grouped around the bubbling water with some little artistic ingenuity; and contrasting in their decay with the active life of the sparkling stream and the never dying light that shone upon them, they formed a picture full of thought and memories for every one who had within him the gift of its interpretation.

Passing on at length with a look such as his countenance never wore except in perfect solitude, bespeaking fatigue, hesitation, and something akin to despair, Rinaldo's step was arrested by the sight of the girl who had attracted him a few hours ago. She was sitting, or rather half lying on the ground behind one of the broken statues which surrounded the fountain, and thus had been concealed from him until he moved further on. Her head and shoulders lay back upon the marble fragment, her hands hanging down in a posture that indicated extreme exhaustion and helplessness. On first observing her Rinaldo imagined that she had fainted, but a closer inspection assured him that the ghastly paleness of her features, as they lay there turned upwards to the sky, was rather the effect of the moonlight than of insensibility.

Stooping down to ascertain her real condition, he saw at once, from her manner of breathing, that she had not fainted, but was asleep. As he stood watching her, and turning over in his mind whether he should not wake her and see her to a place of safety, an expression of pain distorted her features, and she sighed heavily. Expecting her then to wake of her own accord, he drew himself up hastily and stepped aside, fearing to frighten her if she awoke and saw him bending over her. She was soon awake, and with the bewildered look of a person who has fallen asleep in a strange place, she attempted to stand upright. Her strength failed her, and she sat down, or rather fell upon the ground once more.

Seeing her exhaustion, Rinaldo at once came forward, and asked her whether she was not ill and wanted help.

"Not ill," she replied, her voice all the while belying her; "only tired, but I shall be better in a moment."

And again she tried to stand and walk away, but the effort was too great, and but for Rinaldo's help she would again have fallen. He was at his wits' end, attention to fainting women never having been among the duties of his office in the Vatican or elsewhere. No passers-by were near, to give him either advice or assistance. Then a thought struck him. Helping her to seat herself, and to rest against one of the happily placed marble fragments, he hastened to the house where D'Urbino was detained, and astonished the woman, Giudetta by name, who acted as housekeeper to its inmates, by calling for some wine. Being supplied with what he wanted, not without some questionings as to the cause of the demand, he returned to the exhausted girl, and without more ado insisted upon her drinking what he had brought.

"Is the house where you just went a prison, Signore?" asked the girl, some little revived.

Much surprised, as the outer appearance of the building bore no signs of its actual nature, he asked what could possibly suggest the notion to her fancy.

"I saw a gentleman taken there this afternoon by the police, and he has not yet come out again," she replied.

"How come you to know that he has not long ago left the place altogether?" asked Rinaldo, still more surprised. "Have you been watching from that time till now?"

The bright moonlight revealed to him the confusion with which this question was received. After some hesitation, however, she answered him, with an evident wish to avoid the subject.

"I was very tired, and sat down here and fell asleep," she said.

"But what makes you anxious to learn what has become of the gentleman you fancy to be lodged in the supposed prison?" Rinaldo continued.

"He was taking me to my father's house," said the girl.

"Your father's name is —— ?" he asked.

"Giorgione," she replied, "and I am his daughter Francesca."

"Surely you are not the servant of the gentleman you spoke of," he rejoined.

"I sit to him as a model sometimes; that is all," said Francesca, by no means liking the tone in which she was being examined.

"And is it the habit of young ladies to constitute themselves the guardians of the artists to whom they sit?" asked Rinaldo. She looked so miserable as he said this, that he spared her further questioning.

"Well, well," he said, "I will ask you no more; and if you can walk as far as this terrible prison, you shall learn what has become of your friend."

Afraid to say how thankful she felt, Francesca stood up and hastened to follow her new acquaintance. A few steps convinced her that her strength was gone, and it was only through being half led and half supported by Rinaldo, that she was able to reach the house they sought. There arrived, he consigned her to the care of Giudetta, promising a speedy return. When he had re-entered the room where he had left her, he found her submitting to Giudetta's good-natured commands, and recruiting her exhausted strength with a hastily provided meal. When it was ended, at a look from Rinaldo, the housekeeper left them to themselves. Francesca dared not ask the question that she was burning to utter, but the eager pleadings of her looks told her story to the keen and long practised eyes that were fixed upon hers. It was not in Rinaldo's nature to inflict unnecessary pain, even upon one who was unconsciously arousing within him a combination of emotions in which vexation and regret were the chief elements.

"Cavaliere D'Urbino," he said, "will in all probability be released to-morrow morning."

"Then he is not found guilty of anything?" cried Francesca.

"Not that I am aware of," he replied.

"Is he in this house at this moment?" asked Francesca.

"So I understand," rejoined Rinaldo. "But why is it that you are so anxious about all these matters?" he continued, with a suspicious gaze that set the poor girl's heart throbbing as if it would burst.

"I think—I think," she answered, with hesitation, "that my father would be glad to hear about him."

"Is your father acquainted with him?" asked Rinaldo.

"Yes; and he respects him and likes him," said Francesca.

"And you," said he, with the instantaneous quickness of an English barrister, when he strives to draw an admission from an unwilling witness by the terrifying speed of his questions; "you yourself—what do you think about this Cavaliere D'Urbino? Do you, too, respect him, and also like him?"

The ironical tone in which he uttered the word "like," convinced Francesca that her questioner suspected the existence of something warmer than a mere liking, and a flood of tears of shame and distress came to her relief. Rinaldo sat by in silence while her grief partially expended itself; and when she had recovered her composure, summoned Giudetta to his presence, and to her charge committed the still trembling girl.

"A small carriage will be here almost instantly," he added, looking at his watch. "I ordered it to take me outside the walls to-night, but I can wait while it carries you to the house of the mosaic-worker Giorgione."

As he spoke, the sound of wheels announced the expected arrival, and Rinaldo himself conducted Giudetta and her charge to the somewhat dilapidated conveyance. As Giudetta was stepping in, following Francesca, she lingered a moment to listen to Rinaldo's scarcely audible injunction, desiring her to ascertain all she could concerning Francesca herself, and the terms on which she stood towards the young sculptor upstairs.

And thus it was, that when the mosaic-worker was entering his home once more, nearly maddened at the continued absence of his daughter, he was comforted by the sight of Francesca herself, worn and wretched-looking, indeed, but in safety. Nevertheless, his sense of relief was by no means less keen than his astonishment, when he recognised in the driver of the vehicle a man whom he had long known to be in the service of the secret police of the city.

CHAPTER X.

MR. EVELYN'S ACCOUNT OF HIMSELF.

It was close upon midnight when Evelyn, restored by his midnight walk to his wonted good nature, reappeared in Mrs. Sandford's drawing-room. To the excited looks and questions which greeted his entrance he returned only a languid sigh, and threw himself upon the nearest sofa, apparently totally exhausted. The cousins marvelled at his coolness, while Mrs. Sandford, with maternal care, asked him whether he was not unwell.

"My dear Mrs. Sandford," he replied, in the tone of a grievously injured and innocent person, "which do you think is most mortifying to one's vanity; to find one's principles established at the expense of one's comfort, or to have to give up one's principles with a view of ensuring a comfortable existence?"

Mrs. Sandford's only reply to this most unexpected question was simply a stare, betokening a suspicion that the speaker's head was a trifle turned through fatigue and annoyance; Margaret and Helen were equally stricken silent with astonishment.

"What is your solution of the problem, Miss Osborne?" continued the imperturbable Evelyn. "It is just now of peculiar interest to myself."

Margaret said nothing, but almost made up her mind that Evelyn's levity was at least equal to his selfishness, while Helen's impatience could no longer be restrained.

"Mr. Evelyn!" she cried, "only one word, if you please. Is Francesca safe?"

"Pardon me, Miss Sandford," resumed Evelyn; "your question shall be answered without more delay than is necessary. I will explain myself as fast as possible. Never was a man more cruelly made the sport of a perverse destiny than I have been this evening; and my only consolation is, that the great principle of my life has been established to my renewed satisfaction, though at the cost of most serious suffering. In other words, my heart has suffered, but my head is victorious."

"Is Francesca safe or not, Mr. Evelyn?" struck in Helen, now really irritated. Evelyn vouchsafed no reply, but continued:—

"You know my golden rules, never to trouble oneself about anything whatsoever, and to put off till to-morrow everything which one is not forced to do to-day. With unpardonable inconsistency I have violated both of these maxims, and what is the result? If I had remained quiet in this pleasant room, instead of playing the idiot and walking for hours through these dismal half-lighted Roman streets, you would have heard tidings of the excellent mosaic-worker's daughter—by the way, Miss Osborne, she is wonderfully handsome—"

"Then you have seen her," again interrupted Helen.

"Miss Sandford, allow me to remind you of the old Roman proverb, *chi va piano, va sano;* which means, applied to the present subject, that if you had not broken in upon my story, you would have learnt by this time that your protegée, Francesca, has been safe at home for at least an hour."

"Thank God!" Margaret ejaculated, but in the lowest of audible tones.

"If you had suspected all that I suspected, Miss Osborne," continued Evelyn, with sudden seriousness, "your gratitude for her return would be even more fervent than it is. I heartily join in your thankfulness." Then in his old half-cynical manner, he continued:—

"Here have I been rushing frantically, as mad as Don Quixote himself, after a silly girl, and when I return broken-hearted and hungry, I find her quietly crying at her father's side."

"But surely your labour was not thrown away?" asked Margaret, still a little puzzled.

"Every bit of it, I assure you," he replied; "I have had no more to do with her return than you have. Such are the lamentable consequences of being faithless to one's principles; and this is not all. Socrates, as you may have heard, had his good demon, who considerately warned him of impending evils; but I am confident that I have a very bad attendant demon, '*cacodaimon*,' Miss Sandford, though of course you don't understand Greek. I know you understand Latin; but that a young lady should voluntarily learn Greek, passes my utmost conceptions of female depravity."

"You said that you were hungry, Mr. Evelyn," interposed Mrs. Sandford, "there is supper ready, only waiting for your return."

"Ten thousand thanks for your considerateness, my dear madam," he replied. "A little supper will restore to me that most enviable of gifts, a good opinion of myself. Always cultivate such views," he continued, offering his arm to his hostess, whose doubts as to his sanity were by no means dissipated.

"But now as to my attendant demon, or *diavolo*, or *diavolino*, or whatever he is, can anything be more cruel to a man of my principles than to be tempted to start upon a wild goose chase after a girl I had never seen, and then to find myself involved in the confidences of a young fellow who may be clever enough as a sculptor, but who is insane enough to be a revolutionist. Honestly, now, Miss Osborne, is not this a cruel destiny?"

"Cruel or not," said Margaret, laughing, "it has clearly destroyed neither your appetite nor your fluency."

"Then you don't agree as to the *diavolo* or the *diavolino?*" he asked. "You don't see in me the picture of a good man in adversity, struggling with irresistible and infernal agencies. Speaking of agencies, by the way, that reminds me of a certain agency that I have become acquainted with this night, which has shown me more clearly than ever the extraordinary mistake that people make when they get up revolutions. What do you think of my assisting at the execution of a search warrant, Mrs. Sandford?"

"A search warrant!" cried the three ladies, speaking as one voice; while Evelyn, having mischievously roused their curiosity to the utmost, proceeded calmly to finish his supper.

"Miss Sandford," he began, as soon as he found himself sufficiently refreshed; "you were always an advocate for the acquisition of useful knowledge of all kinds, I know."

"Indeed!" replied Helen, "I have been more generally accused of indifference to any knowledge that is simply useful."

"Ah!" said Evelyn, "that depends upon what you mean by 'useful.'"

"Could you not relieve us by first of all explaining what you meant by assisting at the execution of a search warrant?" interposed Margaret. "We can then discuss the subject of useful knowledge at our leisure."

"That is precisely what I was coming to," rejoined Evelyn. "I was on the point of showing how easily useful knowledge can be acquired without any of those fearful processes to which we were subjected in our school-days; only it is necessary first of all to settle what is really useful."

"I suppose tutors of boys and young men are the best judges in the matter," said Helen; "is it not so?"

"They certainly decide as if they were;" he replied. "I only wanted an admission that an acquaintance with the wardrobe of Roman gentlemen is really valuable information. Certainly I was compelled, when at school, much against my will, to learn the names of the various garments which were in use two thousand years ago in this city; and, saving your presence, Mrs. Sandford, it used to strike me that the clothing of former days was of a somewhat scanty description. I am now in a position to express my conviction that in the matter of dress, civilisation has made considerable advances in the Eternal City."

"You still speak in riddles," said Margaret.

"Then I will make myself clear without further prologue," replied Evelyn. "I have this day witnessed the turning out of the wardrobe of the ingenious but grievously dissatisfied personage, of whom I have already spoken to you, and I am satisfied that if the multiplicity and variety of his drapery, to speak of our modern clothing by a most unappropriate name, could have been seen by a Scipio, or a Cato, or an Aurelius, the result would have been the enactment of sumptuary laws, more rigid than any that the world has ever yet suffered under."

"Pray go on, Mr. Evelyn," said Helen, as he paused for a few moments.

"I was present, as I said," Evelyn then continued, "at the searching of the rooms of your acquaintance, D'Urbino, and I am ready to affirm that, though nothing was found to compromise his political character, the catalogue of his clothes is such as would satisfy the desires of the most anxious of modern mothers."

"Was Signor D'Urbino himself present during the pleasing operation?" asked Margaret.

"Far from it!" Evelyn continued, "he was lodged in prison some time before the search was made."

"In prison!" cried the three ladies with one voice.

"In prison, I grieve to say," he replied, "where also I have had the pleasure of spending a portion of the evening myself."

"The pleasure!" cried the three ladies, again in chorus.

"Certainly," continued Evelyn, "if it is a pleasure to drink some very middling wine at the expense of the Government, and to receive a somewhat sharp lecture from a gentleman whom I had intended to lecture soundly myself. Ah! Miss Sandford," he went on, "I see you are incredulous as to the truth of my words. I really *have* been lectured. Whether I deserved it I leave for you to guess."

"Was it Signor D'Urbino who administered the wholesome reproofs?" asked Margaret, with a laugh.

"It was that very indiscreet sculptor himself," replied Evelyn. "Will you believe it, he pretended to treat me as an impostor, and to disbelieve my assertion that you and your aunt are my friends?"

"And pray on what terms did you afterwards part?" inquired Margaret.

"On excellent terms," he replied. "But there was one thing that the Cavaliere said, which a little puzzled me, but which I think you ought to know. I observed, in the innocence of my heart, that you were much interested in the welfare of this unlucky girl, Francesca, and that it was on that account that I was in search of her; upon which, with evident surprise, he assured me that he had rarely heard the girl mention your names, frequently as he sees her, and freely as she talks to him about her acquaintances. You may smile, Miss Osborne, and think that I have found a mare's nest. But I am confident there is something that you have not got to the bottom of."

"I don't quite catch your meaning," said Margaret.

"I mean that there is some reason why the girl never speaks about you to this pugnacious young sculptor. I suppose you have seen the bust he is making of her; or is it a secret rigidly kept?"

"Not the least in the world," replied Margaret; "he told me about it on the very evening that I made his acquaintance, and we are to go in a party to see it, as soon as it is finished. I really hope that he is not seriously involved in any difficulty with the Government."

"He says that he is not," replied Evelyn; "and he fully expects to be released to-morrow."

"You are aware that the bust is not to be a simple portrait," observed Helen. "It is to be an ideal head of Italy, in her present suffering and sadness."

"Oh! that is it, is it?" asked Evelyn. "Nevertheless, if I may judge by the look of the living Francesca, as I saw her just now, in tears, it is an actual portrait, and nothing else. By the bye, Miss Osborne, I hope you don't give in to the absurd cant about beauty in tears. For myself, I think a woman never looks so ugly as when she is crying."

Margaret laughed, and said she had never formed an opinion about it.

"Then I'll tell you what is my theory as

to the origin of the ridiculous notion. A woman who is, or who thinks herself, handsome, never looks in her glass when she is in tears. When she contemplates the pleasing image she is always in a happy mood."

"Go on, I beg you," said Margaret. "Your remarks are so instructive, that we shall gladly hear more of them."

"Then you know," he resumed, "that as a handsome woman always thinks herself the most handsome woman in the world, she never regards the ugliness of the pretty women whom she may see in tears, as conclusive on the question. You see the line of reasoning?"

"It will be clearer if you will favour us with the rest of the process," said Margaret. "So admirable a reasoner and so close an observer should not be deprived of the pleasure of expounding his own views."

"Why surely it's plain enough," answered Evelyn. "A handsome woman never sees tears on that particular countenance which she herself considers the very type and perfection of feminine loveliness. So she assumes that she herself would furnish an exception to the deleterious effect of weeping upon women in general; and she thus is led on to accept the rubbish of small poets and song-writers."

"How do you know what handsome women think of themselves, Mr. Evelyn?" interposed Helen.

"Is it not an accepted fact?" rejoined Evelyn, with an assumption of humility and seriousness.

"Yes!" said Margaret, "like that other accepted fact about the beautifying effect of tears."

"A good hit, Miss Osborne," rejoined Evelyn; "a very good hit. I like to argue with a woman who can give as well as take in a fair fight. With that little dart of yours lodged within me, I will now take myself off." And with that he took his leave.

"Which of us does he like best?" asked Helen, of her mother, as soon as Evelyn had closed the door behind him.

"I should say, that if he cares for either of you, my dear," replied Mrs. Sandford, "it must be for you. He seems very fond of disputing, I think; and certainly it was not the way in which gentlemen paid their addresses to young ladies in my young days. I don't think he has any intentions at all, about either you or Margaret."

"We shall see," observed Helen; while Margaret said nothing. And they parted for the night.

CHAPTER XI.

DONATO.

Left to his thoughts, in the solitude of his prison chamber, it was long before D'Urbino could close his eyes in sleep, or shake off the painful reverie into which he fell. Wondering for a time what would be the effect of his present misadventure upon his future career, his memory went back to the whole course of his past history, and the sense of loneliness, which was the result of the review, was almost intolerable.

Deprived, while still a very young child, first of one parent and then of the other, unable to recall the recollection of any guidance or tenderness, except such as was lavished on him by a sister a few years older than himself, he seemed to have drifted aimlessly into his present life, and still to be without any fixed object for the devotion of his energies. Companions had come and gone, sometimes apparently on the verge of growing into warm-hearted friends. His hereditary income was small, but it had been sufficient to procure him a very fair education, and his habits never having become luxurious, he was not absolutely dependent upon his gains as a sculptor for his daily bread.

Even his alliance with the liberal party in politics was rather the effect of an irrepressible desire for some lofty aim to which he might devote himself, than a deliberate adoption of liberalism as a philosophy or a policy. Towards the dominant clericalism he felt an intense aversion, but it was because it cramped his energies, thwarted his individuality, and condemned him to an unmanly routine of pleasure and money-making. Towards the superstitions of the multitude he was simply indifferent. There are abundant superstitions in matters of art, he thought to himself, which he must tolerate in others, though for himself he must reject them as traditions of the past, resting on no basis of truth or fact. If Canova believed in allegorical statues and Raffaelle painted Jewish men and women in impossible clothings, such as no human beings ever wore, why should we be hard upon people who believe in miraculous images, or upon priests who imagine themselves the channels of supernatural blessings? We are all of us fools, he would say; and our one great misfortune is that we are so seldom in earnest, even in our folly.

Thus he lived a solitary life in the midst of a throng. With the somewhat vagabond ways of a considerable section of the Roman artist world, both native and foreign in birth, he had not the faintest sympathy. When he found himself in the company of men of this stamp, he quietly endured them as long as it was necessary, and then went his way. If nothing in the world satisfied the needs of his heart and understanding, least of all did those wild, eccentric, conceited, noisy, smoking, and often dirty-looking men and youths, whose one practical notion seemed to be the adoption of the principle that the way to understand and carry out the laws of true art, is to adopt an utter unbelief and licence in everything else.

His brother artists of his own standing, as indeed it was but natural, for the most part thought him proud, cold, reserved and selfish, and too fine a gentleman for their society. Some few liked him, but intimacy with him seemed by no means an easy thing to cultivate. To the few distinguished painters and sculptors whose names the visitor associates with living art at Rome, he was but little known. They were old, and he was young, and when once he was supposed to be a partisan of discontented revolutionists, they were apt to be shy of anything beyond the slightest personal acquaintance. The notion that the interests of ancient and modern art and learning would be sacrificed by the triumph of liberalism in politics is so steadily fostered by the clerical party, and is so readily acquiesced in by the great majority of what are called the patrons of art, that a prosperous painter or sculptor may be pardoned, if he closes his eyes to the abuses around him, and trusts that the deluge may not come till his own days in Rome are ended.

And thus it was, that with all D'Urbino's sincere zeal to give to the ambitious work on which he was now working the character of a lofty ideal, it never rose beyond the elevation of a simple portrait. Whether any ideals whatsoever can in reality be more noble things than true and simple portraits of living men and women, is a question he did not think of determining, even as a mere matter of criticism. As a matter of fact, he grew more sensible with every fresh touch that it was not a figure of long-suffering and lovely Italy that he was designing, but a living Roman woman, and that her name was Francesca, and he was provoked with himself more and more, as the conviction of his failure forced itself upon him.

Nor did he in the least comprehend how it was that his hand was at hopeless variance with his intention. He was too little self-inspecting, with all his tendency to reverie and dreaming, to find out that the failure of his aims was due to the simple fact that his beloved Italy was an abstraction, while the superb-looking Francesca was a living woman. When he sought to express the thoughts and emotions of an "Italy," however deeply beloved, he could only draw upon the resources of his own inner nature; when he modelled the features of Francesca, he had the very truth and life before him. As he now sat in his solitude, all these recollections of the past floated before him as a succession of visions, all grey and sombre in their tones, and the night was far advanced when he threw himself upon the bed provided for him, and fell into a troubled sleep.

In the meantime the carriage that had conveyed Francesca to her father's house returned, and after questioning Giudetta as to the information which she had extracted from the girl during the drive, Rinaldo entered it and directed the driver to hasten with all speed to a certain inn some few miles from Rome on the road to Velletri. He was of course provided with the necessary order for passing through the gates at an hour unusual for travellers, and an hour's journey brought him to the Albergo del Sole, a lonely house, frequented only by the poorer inhabitants of its neighbourhood, but reputed to serve occasionally as a place of rendezvous for the more advanced members of the revolutionary party. The visit was evidently expected, as the landlord had not retired for the night, late as was the hour, judged by the way of Italian inn-keepers. He received the salutations of Rinaldo with respect, and without any attempt at conversation, led him immediately upstairs, and throwing open the door of a room at the end of a long passage, asked him to wait for a few moments, when the person whom he came to see would present himself.

The few moments proved to be many minutes, and Rinaldo was beginning to expect some sort of treachery, when a man entered, whose features, manners, and dress betrayed the character of one of those disreputable hangers-on upon society who are to be found in almost every country in the world, and whose vocation is to prey upon the hopes, the fears, and the necessities of men more laborious or more sincere than themselves. After a cold salutation, he sat down opposite Rinaldo, and asked him to what he was to attribute the honour of the visit.

"To more than one cause, Donato," replied Rinaldo.

"If it is the old story, Signor Cameriere," rejoined the man, "you know my terms, and I cannot alter them."

"But they are now so far heavier than they were before, that it is impossible for me to agree to them," said Rinaldo.

"That is not my fault," replied Donato. "You are as well aware as I am that now that I am in danger of my life on this new charge, I am forced to insist upon the conditions I stated to you the last time we met."

"That was three days before the day on which you were to have been hanged," said Rinaldo.

"Your memory is correct," replied Donato. "And to tell you the truth, it was my firm belief that in that interview you were trying to make everything secure for your own ends, supposing that I had really been hanged. Nevertheless, I was confident that if I still kept my own counsel, you would have contrived some means of saving me, even if I had no other friends to rely on but yourself."

"You know, of course, that I had nothing in the world to do with your escape," rejoined Rinaldo.

"Of that I am perfectly well aware," Donato replied; "and I am also equally well aware that you, or those who employ you, would pay me well to tell you how it was that I came to cheat the gallows when you all thought my last hour was come."

"Why, then, do you refuse the offer? Do you know what I should be authorized to promise you for the secret?" asked Rinaldo.

"Certainly not as much as the sum which I expect you to produce in payment for that little morsel of paper which you are longing to possess. Besides, if I revealed the secret, where would be my hope of escape if I ever again found myself in the hands of your bloodthirsty priests and their executioners?"

"Tell me this one thing at least," exclaimed Rinaldo; "is the secret known to one man only, or to many?"

"I shall tell you nothing," returned Donato. "Don't you know enough of the ways of certain persons to be aware that if I betrayed my friend, or friends, as it may be, I should have a knife in my heart before a week was over?"

"But you might leave the country altogether," suggested Rinaldo.

"Yes, most crafty signore," rejoined the other, "I might do so, and thus lose the handsome payment which I am expecting from the excellent Cameriere Rinaldo."

"I have sworn to you," rejoined Rinaldo, with increasing anger and eagerness, "that it is hopeless to expect so enormous a sum from me. I am not a rich man, and have little but my official salary to live upon. With my very utmost savings I could barely have saved enough to make you the yearly payments which at one time you seemed inclined to accept."

"I am a perfectly reasonable man," returned Donato, with unmoved countenance. "It is simply a matter of buying and selling between us. Since I had the bad luck to knock over that scoundrelly priest, and he went off and died, you are aware that I have no choice except concealment within the Roman territory or flight across the frontier. As long as I remain hidden, you still have me within reach when you are prepared to agree to my terms. If I fly, all your chances are gone for ever."

"Supposing I betrayed you, and you were taken again," said Rinaldo.

"In that case you would take me, but you would not take the precious paper that I have to sell you," returned Donato.

"Of course it is of no use to appeal to

any conscience or generosity in you, when you know my poverty," said Rinaldo.

"Conscience! generosity!" echoed Donato, mocking the very voice of Rinaldo, "are you turned fool, or preacher, or play-actor, that you talk to me of such impostures? I tell you plainly, Signor Rinaldo, that I believe not one word of your stories about your poverty. A man in your place and of your experience in the ways of office knows of a thousand ways of making money, besides the wretched salaries paid by a beggarly government. How many bribes have you already taken, Signor Cameriere?"

"Did you ever hear of my taking one bribe?" asked Rinaldo, indignantly.

"Well! no! but what of that?" asked Donato. "You would not be such an idiot as to unfold your private sources of income to a man like me."

"Have I the credit of being grasping or covetous," retorted Rinaldo.

"So far as I know, you have not," rejoined Donato. "You are held to be one of the best of a herd of thieves and tyrants. And so it is that I half believe in the sentimental foolery that makes you so eager for my precious paper."

"Every man for himself," returned Rinaldo. "You don't understand me or my desires. And as to the life you yourself love to lead, to me it would be wretchedness and misery."

"Just so," said Donato, "every man for himself, and according to his nature. I am not a devilish villain, but I must live; and, like every sensible tradesman, I sell my goods at the best price I can obtain. I happen to have something that you wish to buy, and I name my price. Where is the hardship or the wickedness, I ask you?"

"It was devilish hatred and revenge that first of all tempted you to what you have done," cried Rinaldo; "and you drive me frantic when you talk about the past, as if you were now no longer the villain that you were in earlier days."

"Calm yourself, Signore," retorted Donato, with an insulting affectation of superiority. "Bygones are bygones. When I first became acquainted with your sister, I was an honest man. When she rejected me with scorn and insolence, she maddened me, and I had my revenge. But I am an Italian and not a Corsican; and I think men who nurse their passion when they have had their revenge, are fools, and their own worst enemies. I now entertain none but amiable feelings towards you yourself."

"She never scorned or insulted a living thing," rejoined Rinaldo, with a violent effort at controlling the fierce wrath that boiled within him.

"It comes to the same thing," said Donato; "I thought she did, and I acted accordingly. If the end has been that I happen to be in the possession of a certain something that is saleable, am I to throw away my good luck, just because I happen to have mistaken a lady's words and looks when I was a hot-blooded young man? You were not always the dignified and self-possessed personage whose presence is so appropriate in a crowd of fawning courtiers and false-hearted priests."

"It is useless to talk any longer," replied Rinaldo, with a sigh of weariness. "How long do you intend to remain here?"

"That depends upon yourself," said Donato. "The moment I receive what I ask from you, I arrange to cross the frontier."

"But what security have you that your hiding-place will be kept secret?" asked Rinaldo.

"You yourself are that security," said the other; "I trust to it without a doubt."

"Have you anything more to say?" said Rinaldo.

"Nothing," said Donato. "You are wasting your valuable skill, and robbing your employers of the time that you are paid to devote to their service. You had better go back the way you came."

"I will take your advice," replied Rinaldo, and with the look of hopelessness which he had worn all through the conversation, he left the room, summoned the driver of his carriage, and returned to Rome.

CHAPTER XII.

FATHER AND DAUGHTER.

Waking with the early dawn from his troubled sleep, D'Urbino's first thought took the form of a speculation as to the delay that would occur in his release, which quickly merged in a hope that his visitor of the previous evening would not forget to send him tidings of the missing Francesca. He tried the handle of the door of the room, but it was locked, and there was no available means of making himself heard in the house. The window looked out upon a courtyard, and was guarded by strong bars of iron. Nothing but blank walls were visible, and there was nothing for it but to wait with such patience as he could command.

After an hour's waiting, during which the sense of suspense became almost intolerable, he heard the bolts outside the door withdrawn, and the key of the lock sharply turned. It was, however, only Giudetta who entered, with a cup of coffee and a slice of bread. These she laid upon a table, and to his urgent enquiries as to his release, only replied that she knew nothing at all on the subject, and then left him to his solitude.

With all his annoyance and suspense, the coffee and bread were not unwelcome, and he had barely disposed of them, when one of the men whom he had seen below, entered with a letter in his hand, which he presented to D'Urbino, saying, at the same time, that his "Eccellenza" was free to depart. Tearing open the letter, D'Urbino hastily glanced at its contents. "Mr. Evelyn presents his compliments to Cavaliere D'Urbino, and is happy to inform him that the daughter of the mosaic-worker, Giorgione, arrived safely at her father's house last night. Mr. Evelyn trusts that Signor D'Urbino will give him an opportunity to cultivate an acquaintance somewhat inauspiciously begun. He believes that Mrs. Sandford is anxious to thank Signor D'Urbino for his attentions to her daughter and niece at the time of the disturbance yesterday afternoon."

So ran the note.

"A well-bred man enough, I dare say," D'Urbino thought, as he put it into his pocket, and followed the man downstairs. He was not, however, at liberty to leave the house at once, and his conductor showed him into the room where he had been examined by the police agent, and then left him. After a short interval, he was surprised by the entrance of Rinaldo.

"You are free," said the Cameriere, "and I may add that the Government has reason to be satisfied that you are not implicated in the recent outbreak." And with that he conducted D'Urbino, still as much puzzled as ever, into the open air, and left him.

Looking nervously to the right and left, to ascertain whether any passers-by were near enough to notice the fact that for some reason or other he had been within the walls of the prison, D'Urbino bent his steps to his own house. No one seemed to be observing him, and he was soon at home. His housekeeper was at the door, apparently expecting him, and she welcomed him with extravagant expressions of her pleasure at his return, and of her past fears for his safety. He made her a rough reply, and hastened into his studio. Having quickly convinced himself that all was safe, he summoned the much troubled Betta to his presence.

"I understand, Betta," he said, "that of your own accord you pointed out to the police agents, who came here yesterday, the cabinet where I kept my letters and papers."

"Never, never, Eccellenza!" cried the

astonished woman; "they forced me to go with them, while they ransacked the whole place from one end to the other."

"Your falsehoods are useless," replied D'Urbino; "I only tell you this, in order that you may know that my eyes are now opened to your double dealings. Now leave me!" he added, in a tone that assured the discomfited Betta that he was in no mood to be trifled with, and for the first time since she had been in his service, she obeyed without a word of reply.

His next anxiety was to learn what had been the cause of Francesca's delay in proceeding to her home. He found her in conversation with her father, if that may be called conversation in which the speaking is almost all on one side. Evidently something was wrong between them, and her response to his salutations and his expressions of gratification at seeing her safe and well, was at once formal and passionate.

"Is it true, Cavaliere?" asked Giorgione,

as soon as all salutations and inquiries were over, "that you left my daughter yesterday afternoon, before it was dark?"

The angry and suspicious manner in which he put the question, confirmed D'Urbino's belief that there was something unpleasant between the father and daughter.

"As true as that she is now here," replied D'Urbino. "And I have not the remotest idea why she was not with you till a late hour last night."

"You are a man of honour, Cavaliere," rejoined the father, with painful gravity and sadness, "and I believe you. But Francesca will tell me nothing."

"How did you learn that I was not at home till late last night?" Francesca herself struck in.

"I learnt it from a friend of Miss Osborne," he replied, looking up at her agitated countenance with surprise.

"From a friend of Miss Osborne?" echoed

Francesca, bitterly. "Have you seen Miss Osborne to-day?" she added, in a manner that served only to perplex him more and more.

"I am on my way to her and Mrs. Sandford," replied D'Urbino; "but I looked in for a moment to see how you were after the agitation of yesterday. The ladies will, perhaps, be out, if I stay longer, but I should be glad to arrange with you for the next sitting, as soon as I have paid them my respects. So, for the present, farewell."

And with that he hastened to present himself to the Sandford party. He had scarcely received Mrs. Sandford's thanks for the services he had rendered to Helen and Margaret, and was still protesting that they were very slight after all, when Evelyn entered, and straightway seizing D'Urbino's hand, exclaimed—

"Mrs. Sandford! before a word is said, do me the honour to introduce me formally to a gentleman who is so insensible to my merits as to have taken me for an impostor, and is so eccentric as to unite a love for revolutions with a passion for the noblest of the arts."

Mrs. Sandford laughed, and the desired introduction was immediately effected.

"And how is the beautiful Francesca this morning, Cavaliere?" Evelyn continued. "Of course you have already inquired for her. So splendid a countenance is not to be treated lightly. Of course, by-the-bye, you had my note," he added.

"With very many thanks for it," said D'Urbino, prepared to enjoy the oddities of his new acquaintance.

"What are you looking at so attentively, Cavaliere?" rejoined Evelyn. "Are you doubting whether I am the identical person to whom you behaved so extremely abruptly last night? Oh! Miss Osborne, you cannot imagine what a disagreeable thing it is to be made to think ill of oneself. However, I am thankful to say the unnatural state of yesterday is over, and I am again in that truly Christian frame of mind in which I think well of everybody, but above all, of myself."

"Is that your way of applying the maxim that charity should begin at home?" interposed Margaret.

"A very happy idea, Miss Osborne," he rejoined. "I thank you for it, and will make use of it as my own on the first opportunity. But why do you continue the examinations of my features, Signor D'Urbino?" he asked.

"You would make a very fair bust, I think," replied D'Urbino, in a purely critical and quiet tone.

"You think so?" asked Evelyn, evidently a little gratified.

"I do," replied D'Urbino. "What do you think, Miss Osborne?" he continued, observing the attention with which Margaret was listening. But Margaret only looked disconcerted, and made an attempt to turn the conversation.]

"But now as to sculpture in general, Cavaliere," said Evelyn. "It must be a frightfully fatiguing way of spending one's days."

"One must do something, nevertheless, for one's living," suggested D'Urbino.

"There's something in that, no doubt," said Evelyn. "Nevertheless, to my mind, the one grand proof of the barbarous notions of the old Romans was their passion for statues. Conceive the horrible state of society when, as somebody or other says, there were as many marble statues in Rome as there were inhabitants. No wonder it all came to ruin. The empire must have died of premature decay, the result of excessive bodily fatigue. What is your opinion about it, Mrs. Sandford?" he continued, turning to her with the utmost gravity, as if her reply would be conclusive on the matter.

"I don't know," replied that lady, from sheer inability to comprehend the jesting love of paradox and nonsense in which Evelyn delighted.

And thus they chatted on, half in earnest and half in banter, till it suddenly occurred to D'Urbino that he was prolonging his visit to an unpardonable degree, and he started up, with many apologies, to take his leave. An alteration was then agreed upon in the day on which they were all to visit his studio, and he hastened away, fearing that he might find Francesca no longer within doors.

Far less pleasant had been the renewed conversation between the mosaic worker and his daughter.

"I cannot conceive, Francesca, what motive you can have for your secrecy," said the distressed Giorgione, as soon as D'Urbino had ended his flying visit. "And why were you so agitated when the Cavaliere came in? My dearest child," he continued, taking her hand tenderly, "if there is nothing wrong, why will you refuse to tell me how you spent the time since you left D'Urbino? And if there is really anything wrong, surely your father is the person in whom you should trust in your trouble?"

His tender look and tones served only to draw forth a fresh flood of tears, while she returned the pressure of his hand.

"I cannot! I cannot! I cannot!" she cried at last, throwing her arms round his neck, and hiding her face upon his shoulder.

Utterly bewildered, he could only repeat the same things over and over again.

"Consider how strange it all looks, Francesca," he said. "You can give no account of yourself or your proceedings for six or seven hours, and at last you are brought home under the care of an agent of the secret police. What can it possibly mean? You admit that you were not ignorant that D'Urbino was in prison the whole time, and that you had reason to believe that he would be released in the morning. How in the world did you learn all this?"

"There is nothing wrong," she could only murmur in reply.

"Is there anything you are ashamed to tell me?" asked her father.

"There is nothing wrong," she repeated, a little more positively.

"Are you, then, ashamed of something that happened to you, or that you have done?"

Again she buried her face upon his shoulder, and clung to him with a passionate embrace, but she said nothing. Then gently disengaging himself, he held her before him, and spoke in a sadder voice.

"Francesca, what is it?"

But she only hung down her head, trying all the while to throw herself into his arms.

"Francesca," he went on, "we two are alone in the world. Your mother has long been taken from us, and all but you are gone from me."

She shivered as he spoke, every word cutting her to the heart. At last, violently controlling her sobs, she looked in her father's face, and murmured—

"I will tell you, but not now. I am ashamed, but there is nothing wrong."

"Look me in the face, my darling child," he replied, the tears now standing in his own eyes.

She looked him full in the face, but timidly, and yet with a feeble smile, that spoke of undoubting and infinite affection.

"How old was I when she died?" she asked him, almost in a whisper.

"Your mother?" he asked, in the same suppressed voice.

"Yes," she murmured.

"You were two years old," said her father. "But why do you ask me what you have never asked before?"

"I could have told her," replied Francesca; "at least, I think so."

Then with a wild and passionate movement she seized her father's hand, and kissed it again and again.

"I will tell you, too, as soon as I can," she said, lifting her pleading eyes to meet her father's gaze. "But you will let me choose my own time?" giving to her words the tone of a question.

"I am satisfied, my child," he replied. Then kissing her on the forehead, he rose and led her to a seat, and left her, while he himself proceeded to his daily work in silence. After a time she recovered so much of her composure as to begin to note that the morning was rapidly passing away, and that D'Urbino had not yet returned, as he had promised. So she phrased it in her unspoken thoughts. Then she inwardly corrected herself. "It was no promise at all; he only said that he should come in to arrange for a sitting. He has forgotten all about it, of course. Yes, of course he has forgotten it. Why should he remember it? It is only a matter of business; and of course those rich and noble English ladies like to make him talk to them, and of course he likes to talk to them. Why should he not?"

She was still vainly striving to school her rebellious thoughts to obedience, at one moment resolving that she would never more enter D'Urbino's house, and then bitterly complaining of his delay in returning. Then again she would scorn herself for her insane folly in regarding him as anything but a proud aristocrat, whose warmest feelings towards herself could be nothing more than kind-hearted pity. At last, just as she was making up her mind to ask her father to allow her to leave home for a time, and visit some friend far away from Rome, D'Urbino himself appeared, and every resolution vanished.

"You are very much knocked up, Francesca," he began; "I was afraid the fatigue of yesterday would be too much for you. How soon do you think you can give me another sitting?"

"I shall not be able to give you any more sittings at all," she replied.

"None at all?" asked D'Urbino, quite as much puzzled by the tone as by the substance of her reply.

"Yes," she rejoined, "none at all. I think it is better not."

"But, Francesca, consider;" he said. "You will utterly ruin the whole work, which I have set my heart upon finishing without delay."

"You should set your heart upon nothing, Signore," rejoined Francesca. "You will then suffer none of the pains that we poorer people suffer."

"What in the name of common sense are you talking about?" asked D'Urbino, still more puzzled. "Women are changeable creatures enough, as everybody says; but I always thought that you were above these trumpery caprices."

A spasm shot through the poor girl's heart, as he expressed that admiration for her character which she valued far above all recognition of her personal appearance.

"I am a woman," she replied, "and like all women I can suffer. It is better that I should never sit to you again."

"What mischief-making meddler has been putting all this nonsense into your head, Francesca?" he asked, getting angry at her incomprehensible obstinacy. "This is all that idiot Betta's doing, I am sure. She has been frightening you with her follies about the impropriety of your coming to my house. Surely if your father is satisfied, you need pay no attention to the tittle tattle of scandal-loving old women."

"It is better that it should be as I have said," returned Francesca.

"Answer me this one thing, I beg you," he replied. "Is it Betta who has been annoying you, or filling your head with this preposterous prudery?"

"It is not," she answered.

"Then who is it?" he replied. "Has your father changed his mind?"

"Not that I know of," returned Francesca, struggling violently with herself, in her efforts to betray nothing of her real feelings.

"Then what possible objection can you have to come again?" he asked. "Surely you don't wish to do me an ill turn, now that you have done me such real service."

"God forbid!" she exclaimed, with a sudden intensity of tone, while she laid her hand upon her heart, as if she could stay its wild throbbing by force.

He looked at her for a few moments, anxious to read her reasons in her countenance; but all he could see was that she was undoubtedly suffering keenly from some cause or other, and he was the more bewildered because she steadily, contrary to her usual habit, kept her eyes fixed upon the ground.

"You are certainly ill, Francesca," he at last said, in a more sympathising tone.

"I am not ill at all, Signore," she replied. "Pray leave me. You will find some one else to answer your purpose quite as well as I have done."

"That is impossible, Francesca," he replied. "But I shall certainly tell your father that I am sure you are unwell, and ought not to be allowed to neglect yourself. Where is he? I will go and find him at once." And he rose up to put his intention in execution.

"Not for the world, Signore," cried Francesca, starting forward and seizing his arm.

"Are you mad, Francesca?" he exclaimed, as he saw her look of annoyance and terror.

"Yes! I am mad!" she cried, bitterly.

"What would you have me do, then?" asked D'Urbino.

"Leave me, that is all I ask," she replied; "I shall be better when you are gone."

"As you will then," answered D'Urbino. "I used to think you the most interesting girl I had ever seen, and now I think you the most incomprehensible."

"Is it because women are incomprehensible to men, that men despise them so contemptuously?" asked Francesca.

"What in the name of heaven are you driving at, Francesca?" exclaimed he.

"Nothing!" she replied.

"Nothing?" echoed D'Urbino.

"Nothing!" she repeated.

"Then there is nothing more to be said," he replied. And without another word he left her.

CHAPTER XIII.

THE MARCHESE MAKES ENQUIRIES.

JUST about the time when D'Urbino was leaving Francesca to her solitary sorrows, the bright warm sun was tempting a few strollers to linger on the slopes of the Pincio till a rather later hour than those during which Romans think it pleasant to court the wintry air. In one of the least frequented parts of that popular lounge, Della Porta and Henry Noel were walking at that slow pace, interrupted with occasional standings still, which showed that their talk was peculiarly interesting, and was of the nature of an argument, more or less animated.

"With all that I have seen of your fellow-countrymen, Noel," said Della Porta, who had been ingeniously beating about for some way of introducing the subject without awakening the suspicions of his companion; "they are really very difficult to understand."

"You think so?" replied Noel, in the tone of one who was asking a question. "What fresh reasons have you for thinking so just now?"

"Well, to tell you the truth," said Della Porta, "your friends the Sandfords puzzle me a good deal. To my Roman notions, it seems an astonishing thing that those two girls should have gone to hear that ranting preacher in the Coliseum, yesterday, without any chaperon, and with nobody but their old servant and a girl of the bourgeoise to protect them. Surely you don't justify such a thing yourself."

THE MARCHESE MAKES ENQUIRIES. 249

"Certainly not," replied Noel, "if you mean that it was rash and unsafe to go into a crowd; but nothing more."

"You don't think that girls brought up to act so independently would make unsatisfactory wives, if they had to spend their lives among us Italians?" suggested Della Porta.

"It may be doubted," replied Noel; "but why do you ask?"

"Just as a matter of curiosity," said Della Porta. "Sometimes I have a sort of fancy that some day I might meet with an English girl who might attract me; and one likes to be provided against all contingencies beforehand. Besides, you have known Mrs. Sandford and the young ladies all your life, I think you said, one day."

"Not Miss Osborne," replied Noel.

"Miss Sandford seems an amiable girl," said Della Porta, "and I suppose it is only her own fault that she has not long ago made some fortunate man happy."

"I don't know anything about it," rejoined Noel, curtly, and the subject was dropped for a few minutes. As soon as he could adroitly re-introduce it, Della Porta began again:—

"Then you don't think these very independent ways of the Sandfords are inconsistent with perfect refinement and simplicity?"

"You mean something more than you say, Marchese," said Noel. "I have suspected something for some days past."

"Miss Osborne seems a clever as well as an amiable woman," suggested Della Porta.

"So I should think," answered Noel; "but really you know very nearly as much about her as I do."

"And Miss Sandford," continued Della Porta. "What do you think of her?"

With all his effort at appearing indifferent, Della Porta could not conceal the real interest with which he put the question.

"Miss Sandford!" echoed Noel, by no means pleased at Della Porta's persistency in continuing the discussion. "I really cannot inform you what sort of a wife she would make, if that is what you mean."

"Mrs. Sandford seems an amiable and sensible person, I should say," continued Della Porta, not noticing his companion's reluctance to answer his questions.

"Yes," replied Noel, "she is amiable and tolerably sensible. By the bye, have you heard anything more about the fresh excavations at Pompeii."

"Nothing," replied Della Porta, with profound indifference. "How do you English people arrange about mothers-in-law, in such circumstances as Mrs. Sandford's?"

"I can't say exactly," said Noel. "I am told they have discovered some more skeletons of men buried in the torrents of ashes."

"Have they?" rejoined Della Porta. "What do you think Mrs. Sandford would expect to be her own position, if her daughter married?"

"I don't know," returned Noel; "you have heard, of course, of the new ingenious plan for preserving the exact form of the living bodies, of which the skeletons are all that now remains."

"No, I have not," said Della Porta. "Do you happen to know whether Miss Sandford has any fortune of her own, beyond what her mother can give her?"

"She never told me," replied Noel. "It is done by filling up the hollow with hot plaster of Paris, and the effect is wonderful."

"Is it?" said Della Porta. "Judging even by your high English standard, Miss Sandford seems to be a very well educated girl."

"Yes," rejoined Noel. "I am thinking of running down to Naples for a week or two. What do you say to joining me in the trip?"

"Are you?" said Della Porta. "She certainly is a striking and distinguished-looking person; and I never cared much for fair women."

"Indeed!" said Noel. "Which would you rather do; go by rail or by sea?"

"By neither," replied Della Porta; "many people think Miss Osborne the handsomest of the two cousins; but I cannot say that I do. Of course, as being in orders, you have no business to discuss the difference between one woman and another; but as you have known the Sandfords from your boyish days, you might perhaps remember what she looked like when she was younger. Would you say, then, that when she was a girl, she promised to grow up into the very good-looking woman she now is? But, my dear fellow, what is the matter? you really look ill. I have noticed that you seemed out of condition for some days past. Did you not say something about a trip to Naples? If I were you, I would go by all means. You want change of air, depend upon it. Rome's a detestable place to stay in for many months together."

"Well, I suppose I *am* not what I ought

to be," replied Noel, in a strange tone, and with something so like a sigh, that any observer less pre-occupied than Della Porta would have suspected a double meaning in his words.

"By-the-bye," exclaimed Della Porta, suddenly changing the subject, "they tell us that our old acquaintance, Evelyn, is in Rome, and sporting his pretended Epicureanism as vigorously as ever."

"So I hear," said Noel, only too glad to be relieved from the Marchese's evident matrimonial speculations.

And after some more talk on indifferent matters, they went their ways, Noel to his lonely lodgings, and the Marchese to call upon Evelyn.

"Ah! my dear Epicurean," he cried, entering Evelyn's room at his hotel, "welcome once more to the Eternal City," and he griped Evelyn's extended hand with that disagreeable vigour which he considered to be *de rigueur* among Englishmen.

"Epicurean!" echoed Evelyn; "say rather imbecile, or Quixote, or whatever name you think most befitting the most inconsistent and weak-minded of men.

"Yes, I did hear something of your yesterday's exploits from the Sandfords this morning," said Della Porta. "What pleasant people they seem, now one comes to know them more intimately."

"Very pleasant indeed," returned Evelyn. "But they tell me you knew them last winter, and they were always people one could get on with, when once the ice was broken."

"True," said Della Porta, "but they have now an addition to themselves, and in some way or other, the presence of a third person makes conversation easier, and enables one to form a better estimate of people's characters."

The faintest possible smile lighted up Evelyn's features, never particularly grave, but it was gone in a moment.

"You think so," he replied.

"Yes, I do," said Della Porta; "when one is talking to a couple of women, one is forced to talk oneself, either to one or other of them, all the while one is with them. But when there are three, they talk now and then to one another, and so reveal some little of their real characters."

"Perhaps so," said Evelyn, wondering whether there was anything in all this beyond mere critical speculation.

"Miss Osborne, at any rate," replied Della Porta, "is a vast help when conversation flags. I hardly know a better talker, considering her age."

"What on earth is the meaning of all this?" thought Evelyn to himself. Then he answered aloud, "She is a singularly intelligent person, to my judgment at least."

"An old friend, perhaps," suggested Della Porta, "yet I don't remember that I ever heard you mention her in former days, when you used to describe the rest of the family."

"Did not I?" asked Evelyn, wishing to appear totally uninterested.

"At any rate," said Della Porta, "knowing your odd English ways, I used to fancy now and then that I detected incipient signs of a certain *tendresse* towards another young lady, whose praises you seemed never tired of sounding. Do you know it was entirely through your talking so much about them, that I was so anxious to get on a footing of intimacy with the Sandfords?"

"And you did not succeed until quite lately?" inquired Evelyn.

"No," said Della Porta, "for some reason or other, so it was. It is all the work of that charming niece of the very amiable old lady, with whom, to tell you the truth, I find it just a little difficult to keep up any sort of conversation."

"I suppose you see a good deal of them," suggested Evelyn.

"Well, yes, on the whole I suppose I do," replied Della Porta; "but I never could make out whether Miss Osborne is Mrs. Sandford's own niece, or her niece by marriage."

"Her own niece," said Evelyn; "but why do you ask?"

"Oh! I can hardly say," said Della Porta, appearing to hesitate. "One always likes to know the exact relationships of people one associates with. Miss Osborne, too, seems much too clever a girl to have such a very—well, what shall I say?—such a common-place, but doubtless such an admirable person as Mrs. Sandford, for a near relation."

"I don't see that," rejoined Evelyn, "if wise children may be born to foolish parents, why should not clever nieces sometimes have very stupid women for their aunts?"

"Do you think Mrs. Sandford so very stupid a woman, then?" asked Della Porta.

"She seems a very interesting subject of study to you, at any rate," remarked Evelyn.

"It's an old foible of mine, you may remember. In our enforced idleness, we Romans, who are not compelled to work for our own bread, find a relief in these kind of things."

"That is true enough, I dare say," replied Evelyn.

"Then, again, in the same way we like to study the social habits of foreigners more happily placed than ourselves," continued Della Porta. "For instance, I never could quite make out the sort of terms on which aunts stand towards their married nieces and their husbands."

His suspicions now thoroughly roused, Evelyn made no immediate reply. He knew well that the Marchese was a man of perfect honesty and straightforwardness in intention, but at the same time by no means free from that practical trust in *finesse*, which is common to almost all Italians. So to gain time he only said that he did not fully understand his friend's meaning.

"Well then," replied Della Porta, "suppose I put a case, by way of illustration. If Mrs. Sandford married again, on what terms would Miss Osborne consider herself towards her aunt?"

"But you were speaking of nieces who married, not of aunts who married second husbands," said Evelyn.

"You are right," said Della Porta, "supposing—well, how shall I put it?" And with all his diplomatic skill he could not conceal from himself the fact that he was blundering, and that Evelyn was aware of it. "Supposing that Miss Osborne married, how about Mrs. Sandford?" he asked.

"I can't conceive what you mean," replied Evelyn. "How should Miss Osborne's marriage affect an aunt who has her own daughter to live with?"

"It's only mere curiosity, you know," replied Della Porta; "but still an idle man like myself is curious about all sorts of trifles. Suppose we put it another way. If

Miss Sandford were married, would your English ideas about mothers-in-law prevent their all constituting one household? Or would aunt and niece then betake themselves to a separate home? And to speculate further still, how would any man who afterwards married Miss Osborne be situated towards her aunt?"

"I suppose, being all English people, they would fall naturally into English ways," said Evelyn, still in the dark, but by no means liking what he heard.

"Aye, that's true enough, of course," said Della Porta. "But suppose one of them married an Italian? What then?"

"Do you mean Miss Sandford, or Miss Osborne?" asked Evelyn, in so serious a manner that the diplomatic Marchese felt very far from comfortable.

"Neither one nor the other, in particular," he replied. "Perhaps I should make my meaning clearer, if I suppose that both of them will marry Italians."

"The deuce you do!" exclaimed Evelyn, fairly thrown off his balance.

"Why not?" asked Della Porta. "Such things have happened before, and may happen again."

"Undoubtedly," said Evelyn; "only I had no idea that anything of the kind was likely to happen."

"No more have I," replied Della Porta, "strictly speaking; that is, I believe nothing has been actually settled, or perhaps, it would be more correct to say, seriously contemplated. However, at any rate, pray do not pay attention to my random talk."

"Is it all random talk?" asked Evelyn. "Come now, my dear fellow," he continued; "why can't you speak out? I know as well as if you had already confessed it, that you have some meaning in what you are saying. Let us understand one another. Tell me what plan you have got in your head."

Taken aback by this sudden appeal, Della Porta was at first totally at a loss what to

THE MARCHESE MAKES ENQUIRIES. 263

reply. Nervously anxious not to commit himself, and to the last degree dreading anything that might by chance cause annoyance to the woman for whose hand he had nearly made up his mind to negociate, he felt it out of the question to discuss the matter openly with any one. Evelyn himself, he now felt sure, would prove a by no means indifferent confidant, and a premature disclosure of his hopes might create obstacles in his way which he had not hitherto anticipated. On the whole, he had made up his mind that he had better say no more at present. This, however, he quickly found to be impossible. Evelyn's impatience would tolerate no long meditations.

"Well, Marchese," he exclaimed, "how long will you take to decide what to say?"

"On the whole," replied Della Porta, "perhaps I had better say no more to-day. Another day I shall probably trespass on your friendship to do me a little service. In such affairs one can't be too cautious, for other persons' sakes as well as for one's own."

"Unquestionably," rejoined Evelyn. And the subject was exchanged for less personal topics. Evelyn's suspicions were, nevertheless, so thoroughly roused, that on the first opening, he recurred to it, though in a roundabout way.

"The Sandford party seem to have made a good many acquaintances," he observed. "English people don't often get on so well with foreigners as they do."

"They certainly do so," said Della Porta, "I don't exactly know why, but they are undoubtedly generally popular."

"Which of the two cousins should you say, was the most liked?" asked Evelyn.

"That is not an easy question to answer;" said Della Porta. "You know that Miss Osborne is comparatively a stranger in Rome."

"Yes," said Evelyn.

"Yet she is a very striking girl," said

Della Porta; "don't you think so? I suppose she comes here perfectly heart-whole; is it not so?"

"I really am in the dark as to her feelings, my dear fellow," said Evelyn, satisfied that all this questioning was but a preliminary for Margaret's hand. He could, however, think of no more ingenious way of getting at Della Porta's meaning than to turn the discussion to the state of her cousin's affections.

"Miss Sandford has been here for two winters, I think," he said; "would you say the same about her that you imply about her cousin's inclinations?"

"I can only return you your own reply," said Della Porta, suspecting that he was now on the track for discovering what he had begun to imagine as to the real cause for Evelyn's visit to Rome. "I really am in the dark as to her feelings."

"She is a delightful girl, at any rate," said Evelyn. "On that point there can be no doubt, and after all, perhaps, she will marry an Englishman."

"For the credit of the Roman nobility, let us hope that she will not long remain unappreciated among us Italians," rejoined Della Porta.

"She would be appreciated everywhere, I should say," said Evelyn. "But now, returning to my new acquaintance, D'Urbino," he continued; "he seems a plucky fellow, and an accomplished man besides, I should say."

"Yes, he is, as far as I know;" replied Della Porta. "I should not be surprised if he became quite an *ami de la maison* with the Sandfords. Miss Osborne takes to him wonderfully, I fancy."

"Miss Osborne!" echoed Evelyn.

"Yes, why not?" replied Della Porta. "She asked me all about him the first night I met her at the French Embassy ball. You know she is wild about the Roman art of past days, and I fancy she thinks

D'Urbino more in earnest about art and things in general than we for the most are."

"Humph!" growled Evelyn.

"Then she has taken up that handsome girl who lives next door, and who has been sitting to D'Urbino for his ideal 'Italy.' That gives them a common interest."

"I don't understand you," replied Evelyn. "Do you mean the girl or the statue?"

"Well, perhaps both of them."

"What is the girl really like?" asked Evelyn. "I have seen her, as you may have heard; but is she anything more than an uneducated girl. She is not, of course, what we English people mean when we call a girl a lady. I half suspected that D'Urbino had a notion of marrying his splendid model. If so, he might enjoy talking about her to Miss Osborne."

"I know very little of the girl, but if D'Urbino has any hankerings after a *mésalliance*, it is not in that quarter."

"A *mésalliance*!" thought Evelyn, "what

on earth can he possibly mean. A *mésalliance* upwards or downwards." But he kept his interpretation to himself, and only said, "Indeed? I suppose such things are not common among you exclusive Roman nobles."

"They are not common," replied Della Porta, "but such things do occur." And with that the conversation ended.

CHAPTER XIV.

LONELINESS.

WHATEVER were the doubts and perplexities generated in the minds of Evelyn and Della Porta by their cautious questionings and counter-questionings, no such doubt or perplexity distracted Henry Noel, as a result of his talk with the Marchese. Never before had he felt the loneliness of his solitary lodging so utterly miserable, for never before had he been so thoroughly convinced of the one tremendous mistake of his life. The anguish which pierced him through and through, as Della Porta went on unfolding to him by implication his hope that he would one day become the husband of Helen Sandford, revealed in all its terrible reality the fact that the love of his early youth was as living and fervent as it had been when at four-and-twenty years of age he had renounced all thought of her, in order to take orders, and so cut himself off from her for ever.

It was true that he was not certain that Helen was the object of the cautious Marchese's aspirations. His hints and queries had been framed so mysteriously, that it was quite possible that Noel had deceived himself. Still the acute pain with which he contemplated the bare supposition that Helen might be sought and won by another man, was enough to lay bare to him the reality of the affections from which he had until now been habitually turning his eyes.

Bitterly he reproached himself for the folly with which he had suffered himself to be led away by fanatical excitement to take a step which must darken his whole after life. He had often mourned over the weakness which had made him the victim of a temporary enthusiasm, and felt indignant at the existence of a system which could lead men to take leaps in the dark, and imagine that they were thereby accomplishing the divine will. But now that years had passed away, and the full extent of the sacrifice he had made confronted him in all its terribleness, he hated himself, instead of mourning over his weakness, and his indignation against the system which had deluded him burst out into execrations.

For hours he continued going over the whole history of his youth and manhood, and picturing to himself every detail of the circumstances under which he had pledged himself to the priesthood. Again and again he recalled the first beginnings of his passion for Helen, and the rise, progress and victory of the excitement which had led him to imagine that once in orders he would have no difficulty in eradicating every trace of his past love from his heart.

It seemed as if it were but yesterday that he had determined to adopt the fashionable devotional device for deciding upon the life he would choose. Like thousands of others, women as well as men, he had " gone into retreat,"—to use the technical phrase—in order to spend at least a week in endless prayer and meditation, perfectly solitary, except when listening to the exhortations of some ecclesiastic versed in the application of the appropriate stimulants to the excited soul. Then at the end of the appointed period, he had made his choice, and " renounced the world," as he was taught to express it, and devoted himself to the priesthood under the belief that a special illumination from heaven directed him in his decision.

" What madness it all was !" he now cried to himself, as he strode restlessly up and down his room, too agitated to feel weariness. " What a fatal blunder it is to imagine that when the brain is wild with excitement of days and days of incessant praying and thinking, a man is fit to make his choice as to the course of his whole life! How could I be so senseless as to suppose that my love would vanish at my command, just because I thought it would be a grand thing to sacrifice it for a noble end? Ah! I see it all now, as hundreds of others must see it also, when the time for repentance comes. Why did I not see it then? Why did I not see the difference there is between submitting to the irresistible facts of life, as the decrees of Providence, and the choosing my own fate, and then fancying my choice to be the choice of God? Yes! it was a delirium and nothing else. I was drunk with the spiritual excitement which was the natural consequence of those days of solitude, and was no more capable of looking backwards or forwards calmly and like a reasonable being than if I had been maddened by wine."

And he flung himself upon a chair and buried his face between his hands, his whole frame shaking with the violence of his emotion. Then he began again his restless pacing to and fro.

"And all this while," he went on saying in his thoughts, "I have been living in a fool's paradise; thinking that I felt towards her only a brother's love, but secretly trusting that no man would ever take her from me, and I could sun myself in her friendship for my whole life. Why have I been fool enough to encourage her in her pleasant ways, and not see that I was only helping her to mix the poison which I must some day drink? Why did I not fly the moment she came here again, after years of absence from her? Why did I indulge my wish to see for myself whether she had really grown into the brilliant woman they told me about? And why am I at this moment hoping that it is all a mistake about this man's love for her, and that she may still continue my very dear friend and sister? Yes; friend and sister, such as friend and sister never was before! And all the while, there is no love for her in him, and such as he is. It is all cold-blooded bargaining. I could give her up to a man worthy of her, if he loved her as madly as I have loved, and as I know that I love her now. But to give her up to a frozen-hearted dandy who will chaffer for her with her mother, as he would chaffer with a picture-dealer for a fresh ornament for his palace! Oh, my God! why hast thou laid this punishment upon me to bear?"

And he threw his arms upwards in his agony, his hands clenched and every feature in his countenance strained with a frightful tension. Then he fell upon his knees, and a flood of tears came to his relief.

He had scarcely attained a partial calm, and was vainly trying to occupy his thoughts with the first book that came to hand, when a visitor was announced, and to his surprise and annoyance, the Cameriere Rinaldo entered the room. At any other time the visit would not have been unwelcome, as Noel felt none of that antipathy towards Rinaldo which was entertained not only by the Roman Liberals, but even by some persons in the papal household itself. Whether or not there was any truth in the popular suspicion which fixed on Rinaldo the reputation of a spy, Noel could not tell. Certainly he was conscious of no sentiment of personal dislike towards the Cameriere. There had never been very much intercourse between them, and that which had taken place had been for the most part of an official kind, and connected with the duties which until quite recently, Noel had discharged in connection with the Roman university. But, so far as this intercourse had gone, it was plainly not unpleasant to either of the two men; and, though to a scarcely appreciable extent, was tinged with the friendship which distinguishes the manner of a father and a son who are on good terms with one another.

At the present moment, however, all that Noel desired was solitude, and he received Rinaldo's greetings with an unwillingness that he took no pains to conceal. As it happened, Rinaldo's business was of an official nature, and required a certain amount of detailed explanation and discussion which could not be avoided. It was nearly concluded when Noel felt Rinaldo's eyes fixed upon him with a sympathetic expression.

"You are ill," suddenly exclaimed Rinaldo. "I saw that something was wrong when I came in, and the talk has been too much for you; pardon me if I ask you if there is any possible service that I can render you?"

Noel shook his head, and tried to assume the tone of one prepared for any amount of business conversation.

"I am an old man," continued Rinaldo, "and you are a young man. Is there anything in which the results of my experience may be of use to you?"

The offer would have seemed an impertinent intrusion into his private affairs, and possibly a mere trap for the discovery of political secrets, were it not for the manner of the speaker, and the look of kindly interest which Noel read upon his features.

"If you are what they say," he thought, "you are the most consummate actor in all Rome; and we have actors by the hundred among us." And when he replied, declining the offered assistance, it was in so grateful a tone that Rinaldo repeated the offer more urgently.

"I said I was an old man," he went on, "but though I am old enough to be your father, I am hardly what people call aged, except in the long and painful knowledge acquired in a lonely life."

"Do you think, then, that there is no knowledge, except that which is painful, to be acquired by those who are condemned to loneliness for their whole lives?" said Noel, finding himself impelled, against all his efforts, to continue the conversation.

"That depends upon the original cause of a man's loneliness," said Rinaldo.

"Suppose it is the consequence of one's own mistake," said Noel.

"Even then there would surely be vast differences between one case and another," replied Rinaldo.

"Supposing it had involved some heavy sacrifice, to which a man found it impossible to reconcile himself in his cooler moments ever afterwards?" suggested Noel.

"You mean, I gather from what you say," rejoined Rinaldo, "that after such a sacrifice and such a mistake, the whole of life must be so clouded with wretchedness, that every pleasure must be embittered, and every pain intensified."

"Something of the kind," replied Noel.

"Such loneliness would indeed be miserable," rejoined Rinaldo; "I can conceive few conditions of life more hopelessly melancholy. But there may be worse loneliness than this."

"Is it possible?" asked Noel.

"Very possible indeed," said Rinaldo; "the blunder which you describe does not necessarily involve an utter severing of all human ties. There are men who live in a crowd, and know that no human beings would care if they dropped dead at their feet, except from the unpleasantness of the shock to their nerves."

"There are not many such men, I should suppose," rejoined Noel. "Everybody must have some friend, or some kinsfolk, in whose heart he holds a place. Life, absolutely without love of any kind, must be a living death."

"It is," replied Rinaldo.

"Surely, Signor Rinaldo," rejoined Noel, struck with the increasing sadness of his visitor's manner, "surely you do not mean that this is the result of your own personal knowledge of life."

"That living death is mine," replied Rinaldo.

"I know what people say of you," rejoined Noel; "but is it true that you have no living being who cares for you? Have you absolutely no friend in the world?"

"Not one," said Rinaldo.

"And not one single relation who owns the tie of blood, if none others?"

"Not one that I know of," said Rinaldo.

"What object, then, do you live for?" asked Noel, secretly thanking God that his own loneliness was not like this.

"I do not live," said Rinaldo, "I exist; but I am so weary that it would be a mockery to call my round of nights and days by the name of life."

"And you have nothing before you that you wish to accomplish before you die," suggested Noel.

"I had one once, but I begin to despair of attaining it; and it might as well have no existence," answered Rinaldo.

"Then why do you condemn yourself to the strange duties which report assigns to you?" asked Noel.

"Report is a liar everywhere, and in Rome a more habitual liar than elsewhere. I have no duties but those of my recognised post."

"Aye," replied Noel, "but what are the duties of that post?"

"You ask me why I accepted the post," said Rinaldo; "I will tell you: partly by way of increasing my income, and partly in the hope of attaining the one only aim of my life."

"Yet you continue to hold the post now that you have given up all hope of gaining your object. How is this?" said Noel.

"The condemned criminal will eat and drink almost on his way to the gallows," replied Rinaldo; "and thus even in despair I still live on and hope in vain."

"And is this lonely life the result of your own deliberate choice?" asked Noel.

"Not in the slightest degree," said Rinaldo; "I drifted into it helplessly. Circumstances have been too strong for me, and it is the result also of the radical defect of my natural character."

"What is that?" asked Noel, astonished at finding himself the recipient of the confidences of a man to whom he had always attributed an iron reserve.

"I am a feeble man in action," said Rinaldo, "because I so habitually see the arguments both for and against any definite course, that I vacillate till the time for all real choice is gone."

"I have heard of such a temperament," said Noel, "but you are the last man to whom I should attribute it."

"It is, and always was mine," rejoined Rinaldo. "I was once a Liberal, and yet I was not heartily a Liberal. Now I am what you English people call a Tory, but there is no heart in my Toryism. Thank God that you are spared this miserable disposition, at any rate."

"I wish to God that I had been more in love with indecision when I was younger than I now am," exclaimed Noel, bitterly. "You, at any rate, are spared the misery of actively ruining your own life."

"It comes to the same thing, nevertheless," replied Rinaldo. "Of course I guessed from your first questions to me that you were speaking of some terrible mistake of your own, and now I know it. There can be but one explanation of it all. You regret that you entered the priesthood."

Noel made no reply, but hung down his head in silence.

"And the sacrifice has been too great for your future peace of mind," Rinaldo continued, but Noel still said nothing.

"You may yet regain it," Rinaldo went on. "There are worse miseries than an enforced celibacy. A mistaken marriage is a still more terrible doom."

"I am thinking of going away for the winter," replied Noel, when at last he felt it necessary to speak.

"Indeed?" exclaimed Rinaldo, as if such a project was unaccountable. "It was only a few days ago that you happened to mention that you had old friends coming for the winter."

"They are come, but it does not alter my plans," said Noel, hesitating how to express himself. "They were here last winter, you may perhaps remember."

"Surely your friends are not the English mother and daughter who were at Tivoli that morning when I first made your acquaintance," said Rinaldo.

"Yes, the same," replied Noel.

"Then, my dear Noel," said Rinaldo, leaning forward and gently laying his hand on Noel's shoulder, "you are right not to stay."

"How can you possibly know anything about it?" rejoined Noel, almost angrily.

"Your secret is as safe with me, Noel," replied Rinaldo, "as if you had never revealed it."

"What secret?" exclaimed Noel, by no means propitiated by the kindness of Rinaldo's tone.

"The secret of the sacrifice you made when you decided to take orders," said Rinaldo. "I suspected it when we met that day at Tivoli. Come, now," he added, "I will not speak a needless word to distress you. It was impossible to see you in company with the young lady in question, and not discover the false position in which you had placed yourself."

"And you have never hinted your suspicions from that day to this?" asked Noel, a little mollified, but bitterly annoyed.

"Never," said Rinaldo. "I have lived a lonely life, as I have told you; but it has not yet hardened me to other men's troubles. If I have any one virtue, it is the faculty of holding my tongue, and now remember this, that for the sake of the lady herself, you are bound never to betray, either to her, or to any living creature, the secret of your past mistake. You must not trust yourself in her company until all remains of your old passion are dead within you. Others beside myself may guess something from your treacherous eyes, and the uncontrollable movements of your restless lips; and you know enough of an ill-natured world to understand that it will not believe that the passion has been, or still is, all on one side."

"It has never been on hers, I firmly believe," murmured the unhappy Noel, unable longer to keep up his poor attempts at deception.

"That I am sure of myself," said Rinaldo. "No girl would have talked to you as did Miss Sandford on the day when you betrayed yourself to me, who had ever entertained towards you any feelings but those of simple friendship, or who suspected what you really felt towards herself."

"That is my only consolation," said Noel, "it is little, but it is something."

"Is it not a consolation, too," replied

Rinaldo, "to have some one whose happiness is dear to you, and on whose behalf you have a clear duty to accomplish, however cruel are the pangs it costs you? No man's heart need be utterly broken who has before him so noble, even if so painful a task. As for me, I have no one to live for, not even to suffer for; and now there is my hand. I shall see you, I hope, before you go."

And the grasp with which Noel replied to the friendly words showed that they had not been spoken altogether in vain.

END OF VOL. I.

www.ingramcontent.com/pod-product-compliance
Lightning Source LLC
Chambersburg PA
CBHW032054230426
43672CB00009B/1589